PRAYERS FOR HEALING

Other books by John Gunstone

The Feast of Pentecost
Christmas and Epiphany
A Commentary on the New Lectionary (2 vols)
Greater Things than These
The Charismatic Prayer Group
The Beginnings at Whatcombe
A People for His Praise
Pentecostal Anglicans
Live by the Spirit
The Lord is our Healer

PRAYERS FOR HEALING

JOHN GUNSTONE

HIGHLAND BOOKS

This edition 1987

Printed in Great Britain for
HIGHLAND BOOKS
Broadway House, The Broadway
Crowborough, East Sussex
by Richard Clay Ltd, Bungay, Suffolk
Typeset by CST, Eastbourne, E. Sussex.

CONTENTS

NOTES

1 Except where otherwise stated, all quotations from the scriptures are taken from the *New International Version of the Bible* (Hodders, 1986)

2 The prayers are referred to according to their number in each Part, e.g. 3.9 = Part 3 prayer 9.

3 In the texts of the prayers, the words printed in **bold** are to be said by thc congregation.

ACKNOWLEDGMENTS

The quotations from the *New International Version of the Bible* (1986) are reproduced with permission from Hodder and Stoughton. The prayers from *Ministry to the Sick* (1983) on pages 142 and 179 are reproduced with permission from the Central Board of Finance of the Church of England. The excerpts from the English translation of *Pastoral Care of the Sick: Rite of Anointing and Viaticum* (1982) on pages 145–159 are reproduced with permission from the International Committee on English in Liturgy, Inc.

INTRODUCTION

This is a book about offering prayers to God for healing. I wrote it with various Christian people in mind.

First, there are individuals and families who pray for healing when an illness or an accident affects them. Asking the Lord to heal ourselves or someone in the house is the simplest and most obvious form of this ministry; yet many Christians find this difficult to do in their own homes among those they love. Maybe the prayers in Part 1 will help them to get started.

Second, there are the increasing number of Christians who find themselves led to pray for healing in informal situations like house groups and weekend conferences, but are not sure what they should say. I hope the prayers in Parts 2 to 5 will serve as examples for them.

Third, there are those who want to pray more deeply about the ministry of healing, especially through reflection on the scriptures to discern the will of God and the barriers we put up between ourselves and God's healing grace. I have provided in Parts 6 to 8 illustrations of how to examine our lives and how to meditate on passages of the Bible.

Fourth, there are clergy, ministers and lay leaders whose congregations and groups are being nudged by the Holy Spirit to engage more effectively in the ministry of healing, using the spiritual gifts which he provides within all Christian communities. Part 9 contains a selection of prayers from contemporary liturgies, showing how the ministry of reconciliation and the laying on of hands and anointing the sick are provided for in different churches.

In Part 10 I have written out a service of prayer for healing, complete with an outline sermon, directions and other explanatory notes, for a congregation or group which is embarking on this public form of ministry for the first time.

Except where I have used liturgical texts, all the prayers are my own compositions. Some of them have been used by individuals and groups in ministries of healing at home, in church and in hospital. The appendix illustrates how the traditional shape of the collect can sometimes help us in our spontaneous prayers.

The prefaces to each Part have been kept brief, since this is not intended to be a discussion about the ministry of healing; for this I refer you to my *The Lord is Our Healer* (Hodders, 1986). *Prayers for Healing* is a practical and pastoral handbook for what I wrote there.

One risk I've had to take in writing this book is that of giving the impression praying for healing depends on saying the correct things. I know such a suggestion sounds ridiculous, but it's surprising how often that notion seems to lie behind some of the questions people ask when they have prayed for the sick: "Do you think I said the right thing?"—"Would he have got better quicker if I'd left out, 'If it be your will, Lord'?" – "Should I pray for healing if I don't have a gift for it?"

I want to affirm as emphatically as I can that what matters in the ministry of prayer for healing is what God does. Our role in that ministry is to trust him and to cooperate obediently with him. We should expect the

Holy Spirit to lead us and equip us with everything we need to fulfil God's will when we pray with others for their healing—and then get on with it, leaving the outcome to him.

However, there are certain guidelines to help us discern the Lord's will when we pray for healing, and I want to list them as a background to the prayers in this book. They are relevant both for those who pray for themselves when they are ill and for those who pray for others.

GUIDELINES

(1) Believe the scriptural teaching that God wills all women and men to be made whole—to be saved.

The scriptures reveal that God willed his creation should enjoy all possible goodness. "God saw all that he had made, and it was very good" (Gen 1.31). We also know from the scriptures that sin and suffering are the consequences of man's disobedience to God (Gen 3. 17ff.). But although God is able to use suffering and even death for his purposes—supremely through the passion of Jesus Christ—there is nothing in the New Testament to suggest that he does not want the sick to be healed.

Jesus waged a holy war against sickness. It seems that people did not even have to accept his Gospel in order to be healed. "He welcomed them and spoke to them about the kingdom of God, and healed those who needed healing" (Lk 9.11). Never once did Jesus tell anyone that it would be better for them to suffer and to accept their afflictions as the Father's will for them. Never did he utter a beatitude for the sick or for those who suffer physically—only for those who suffer persecution (Mt 5.10).

Christ healed out of compassion, and that compassion was an expression of the divine love revealed through his incarnate life. That love does not change. God still wills sick women and men to be healed and made whole. It is in this belief that we offer prayers for healing today.

Of course, one day we will not be cured in the physical sense. We shall die. For many of us death will come because of some ailment which was not cured. Yet that does not mean that ultimately we shall not be made whole. God is merciful. "We believe that Jesus died and rose again and so we believe that God will bring with Jesus those who have fallen asleep in him" (1 Thes 4.14). Our full healing—our salvation—is the other side of death.

(2) Minister to people where they are.

Many Christians have very little faith in prayers for healing—particularly when they are ill themselves! Even those who have a strong faith in God in other respects can still have doubts about the Lord's ability to heal. Much Christian teaching has been so dominated by the scientific and secular atmosphere of our contemporary society that it is difficult for us to accept that we might be healed through prayer.

Begin by listening to those who ask you to pray with them. Don't try to answer their fears by glib explanations or quotations from the Bible, and don't react to their doubts by trying to stress your own faith. As you listen, the Holy Spirit may begin to show you how you should pray with them. The things they say and the thoughts that flow through your mind may open up for you prayers of petition, confession and praise which are appropriate for that person at that moment.

Accept that you won't be able to answer the questions put to you about why God allows suffering. Acknowledge that in praying for healing we are involving ourselves in the mystery of God's saving purposes for us in Jesus Christ, and that often we are in the dark about how those purposes are being worked out.

Instead, encourage those you pray with to be open to receive whatever the Lord has for them, and remind them that God loves them. This is the fundamental biblical revelation which is the basis for all that we do in Jesus' name. Out of that revelation comes our faith in God, and faith and hope are built up as people experience the love of God through others. The hymn to God's love which Paul inserted into his teaching on the exercise of spiritual gifts is especially relevant to us when we pray for healing:

> Love is patient, love is kind. It does not envy, it does not boast, it is not proud. It is not rude, it is not self-seeking, it is not easily angered, it keeps no record of wrongs. Love does not delight in evil but rejoices with the truth. It always protects, always trusts, always hopes, always perseveres (I Cor 13.4–6).

(3) Trust in the healing ministry which Jesus Christ continues through his church.

Jesus sent out his disciples in pairs with the command: "Heal the sick . . . and tell them, 'The kingdom of God is near you'" (Lk 10.9). After his resurrection he gave them authority to continue the ministry of proclaiming the Gospel and healing the sick, and the Acts of the Apostles recounts how they fulfilled that commission

(3.7, 5.16, etc.). Paul taught that among the gifts of the Spirit were charisms of healing (I Cor 12.9), and James gave instructions about ministering to the sick through prayer and anointing (5.14–16). Undergirding this ministry was faith in the Lord who had promised his disciples, "I will do whatever you ask in my name, so that the Son may bring glory to the Father" (Jn 14.13).

It is true that the church has often been confused about how she should minister to the sick through prayer. At different times and in different places her members have disagreed in their understanding of Christ's commission. In this scientific age many have assumed that the only real healing ministry is fulfilled by the medical and nursing professions, and that the church's job is to stand by them and their patients prayerfully and encouragingly.

Looking back on the story of the church, however, we can see that when her members are renewed in their faith, then the ministry of healing comes to the fore in her mission once again. So it is that through the charismatic renewal and other movements of faith in recent years, more Christians have come to expect God to heal directly in answer to prayer.

(4) Learn from what God is doing in the church now.

There is plenty of evidence in Christian groups, communities and congregations to encourage us in this ministry. Services of prayer for healing are becoming widespread. Testimonies abound—not least in the many books published nowadays on this subject. We can witness for ourselves that the Holy Spirit brings gifts of healing through the body of Christ when God's people call on him in faith.

When prayer for healing is offered, people encounter the grace of Jesus' healing touch in various ways. Sometimes a remarkable—even miraculous—cure, astonishing the doctor as well as the patient's relatives and friends. Sometimes a rapid recovery in convalescence. Sometimes an inner healing of attitudes and relationships. Sometimes an acceptance of death as the door to complete healing. Such are the signs of the kingdom of God manifested through this ministry.

We can never stop learning. Take any opportunity offered to you to attend courses and to join in ministry with others more experienced than yourself. Nearly everything I know about the ministry of healing I've picked up through seeing how others went about it. And some of the best advice I've had has come from members of the medical and nursing professions who have shared in ministry to the sick with me.

(5) Seek the Lord's forgiveness for sin and be ready to forgive others.

Salvation is moral and spiritual: it relates to a deliverance from sin and its consequences, including sickness. That is why some healings in the New Testament were linked with the forgiveness of sins (Mark 2. 1–12; John 5.1–15).

The scriptures reveal that sickness and sin are strangely enmeshed together, one interacting on the other. It may not be the sinfulness of the individual concerned which is at the root of his illness (and we certainly should not give the impression we think it might be). It may be disobedience to God within the church of which he is a member, or the rejection of God's law by the society of which his church is a part. But no healing can be complete without healing from the effects of sin, whatever those effects might be.

Then, too, some folk need inner healing before they can reach out in faith for what the Lord is offering them. A few may require deliverance from strange spiritual bondages.

From the viewpoint of the Gospel, healing is a sign of the salvation which God offers us through Jesus Christ. Since sickness, with sin, is evidence of the power of Satan, then healing, with forgiveness, is evidence of Christ's triumph over him. This triumph was unfolded through Jesus' earthly ministry, particularly in the healings he bestowed on those with diseases and the liberations he brought to those who were possessed by demons. That ministry reached its victorious climax in his death and resurrection (I Cor 15.20–28).

But healings are not a guaranteed by-product for all those who turn to Jesus Christ in repentance and faith. We can be no more certain that we shall be completely healthy than that we shall be completely sinless. Yet we know from the scriptures that when we have repented of our sins, confessed Jesus Christ as our Saviour and Lord, been baptised, and received the Holy Spirit, then we are to count ourselves dead to sin but alive to God in Christ Jesus (Rom 6.11).

(6) Discern the different ways in which God heals.

Many natural gifts are exercised in the healing of people, from the body's own resources to the wonderful results of medical science and nursing care. When we see others involved in caring for and curing the sick, we acknowledge that they, too, are agents of the Lord's healing, even if some of them do not personally recognise it.

"Honour the physician with the honour due to him, according to your need, for the Lord created him; for healing comes from the Most High. . . The Lord created medicines from the earth, and a sensible man will not despise them" (Ecclesiasticus 38.1–2, 4).

Therefore we should respect the opinion of a patient's doctor when we ask how to pray for healing. I do not mean that we should always let his opinion limit our hope in what the Lord might do. By its very nature, medical science has to abide by the results of its own research and experience. It cannot take into account acts of God's sovereign will beyond what is regarded as scientifically feasible. But at least we can listen to what the doctor has to say. His diagnosis and prognosis can be a starting-point for our prayers. And we can invite him to pray, too.

Respect for a patient's doctor also means that we should be extremely careful in making claim for healings when there is no medical evidence to support those claims. In the current renewal of the ministry of healing, much damage is being done by people who report cures when no real cure has taken place. It is even worse when those who have been prayed over are told they are healed when they haven't been. On two or three occasions I've attended services of prayer for healing with friends who are doctors where certain persons received the laying on of hands as prayers were offered for them. Afterwards it was announced that they had been healed. But my friends (who as faithful Christians were longing to witness such spiritual gifts) were sadly unconvinced by the evidence before their eyes.

We do not honour God by exaggerations. It is more honest to report that someone we have prayed with was "feeling better" or "showing signs of improvement" than to say he was "healed" (unless an extraordinary healing has clearly been given or has been medically authenticated).

But, on the other hand, medical science and nursing care do not have answers to all physical, mental and emotional disorders. Sicknesses springing from spiritual troubles can only be dealt with by those who act with the Lord's spiritual authority. And if only a physical cure is effected, leaving other areas of a person's life in an unhealthy state, then the healing is incomplete. God's healing is total—in body, mind and spirit. A good test of any treatment is to ask the question, Does it help the sick person towards the recovery of a life in which he is able to grow in the love and service of God and of others?

(7) Respect the pastoral leadership of your church.

This is not always easy, especially if the pastoral leadership is unsympathetic towards the idea of praying for healing. Some of the men (and a few of the women) who are leaders in the churches today learned their theology in the 'sixties and 'seventies, when it was fashionable to question anything that could be labelled as supernatural, both in the Bible and in contemporary Christian belief and practice. The suggestion that God can and does intervene in his world to heal was regarded as highly unlikely.

If you have a minister or a group of elders/deacons who are sceptical, be very patient with them. When an opportunity to pray with the sick arises, make sure you keep them informed and, where possible, involve some of them with you in the ministry. I have known a number of clergy who have been introduced to praying for healing—and consequently found their own ministry transformed—as a result of the initiatives taken by two or three members of their own congregation.

One of the responsibilities of the pastoral leadership is to coordinate the exercise of different spiritual gifts in a congregation, and those who have a ministry of prayer for the sick should be willing to accept this coordination. "We ask you, brothers, to respect those who . . . are over you in the Lord" (I Thes 5.12).

(8) Beware of deceit.

The exercise of spiritual gifts in and through a Christian group, community or congregation nearly always evokes, sooner or later, manifestations of evil. Sometimes the manifestations may take the form of quarrels or divisions among those involved; at other times they may come as false teaching or unrepentant clients.

Be wary of those who seek to minister, (a) who are not under any acknowledged authority in their church, (b) whose moral lives belie their Christian discipleship, (c) who appear over-concerned about their rewards (reputation, publicity, finance), and (d) who see the solution to every problem in terms of casting out demons.

We live in an age when, because of the development of communications, there are many itinerants visiting churches on a ministry of healing ticket. Some of them are much used by God and we can praise him for their ministries; but some are not.

If you are not sure about someone—either as a teacher or as a person in need of ministry—avoid committing yourself. Give yourself time to think and pray about the individual or the situation. Seek the advice of others, especially those who exercise pastoral leadership or who have more experience than you have in this ministry. Wait for the Holy Spirit to guide you or to provide the answer to the problem. Often we make mistakes when we rush into things with the anxiety that if we don't act now, we may be too late.

The Lord longs to be gracious to you;
  he rises to show you compassion.
For the Lord is a God of justice.
  Blessed are all who wait for him! (Isa 30.18)

(9) Pray at the foot of the cross.

We are saved by the blood of Jesus Christ (Ac 20.28; Rom 3.25, &c.). As this message is proclaimed, and as women and men hear it and respond to it, God's salvation is brought to them (Rom 10.8, 14ff., &c.). The ministry of healing is within the orbit of this saving work, and so we need to remember that our prayers for healing are offered at the foot of the cross.

This helps us in all kinds of situations, but especially when our prayers do not seem to be answered. Such are the conditions of living in this sinful world that even though God does not will us to suffer, suffering and death are inevitable for all of us. What the Father offers us through the Spirit is communion with the Son in his suffering and in his victory.

"We also carry around in our body the death of Jesus, so that the life of Jesus may also be revealed in our body. For we who are alive are always being given over to death for Jesus' sake, so that his life may be revealed in our mortal body" (2 Cor 4.10–11). Paul was writing of what he suffered as an apostle of Jesus Christ—the preaching of the Gospel involved him in dangers and persecutions. But the same principle applies to those who suffer through illness: that suffering, too, can reveal the life of Christ when it is transfigured by God's grace.

Sometimes it takes the form of a miraculous triumph

over continual pain and disability, so that the power of the Holy Spirit in the sufferer points others to Jesus Christ. At other times it is manifested through a faith in God which leads to a peaceful death. To pray for healing without facing the passion of Christ is to seek what is known as "cheap grace."

The cross shows us that God is on the side of those who suffer and die. He is not detached from the problem. It lies within the mystery of his purposes for us. And at the foot of the cross we can affirm, with Job,

> I know that you can do all things;
> no plan of yours can be thwarted. (42.2)

(10) Come to God the Father through Jesus Christ rejoicing in the Holy Spirit.

Always our approach to God should be one of thanksgiving and praise. In one sense we all need healing because none of us is yet perfect in his sight. But in another sense the healing we need has already been accomplished in Jesus Christ. He died for us and included every need of ours in what he did—including healing for our infirmities as well as forgiveness for our sins.

That is why we can thank God in our prayers for healing. Indeed, all intercessory prayer, like all Christian living, should begin and end in praise: "Whatever you do, whether in word or deed, do it all in the name of the Lord Jesus Christ, giving thanks to God the Father through him" (Col 3.17).

Even when the answers to our prayers do not immediately seem to be what we had hoped for, we can still praise him. That is because we know that nothing can separate us from his love. Thanksgiving is an expression of our faith in him: "Through Jesus, therefore, let us continually offer to God a sacrifice of praise—the fruit of lips that confess his name" (Heb 13.15). Deep in the heart of Christian prayer, whatever our circumstances, is the joy and peace which is the sign of the Spirit's indwelling. And without that indwelling of the Spirit, there can be no Christian ministry of healing.

PART 1

PRAYERS FOR HOME AND HOSPITAL

Praying for healing is a form of petitionary prayer; and petitions are the simplest means of approaching God through Jesus Christ. Our Lord encouraged his disciples to believe that the Father would give them whatever they asked in his name (Jn 15.16). Obviously there is nothing automatic about this. To pray in the name of Christ is to pray with complete openness to the Holy Spirit and with faith in the will of God. And if our prayers are not apparently answered as we had hoped, then we are still to trust him, knowing that in all things God works for the good of those who love him, who have been called according to his purpose (Rom 8.28).

Christ's presence was promised where two or three come together in his name (Mat 18.20). The most common grouping of Christians is in the family. The union of a husband and a wife reflects the unity of Jesus Christ and his people (Eph 5.32). With their family the spouses form a "little church". But there are other kinds of families as well: relatives or friends who live together, members of religious communities, a group of Christian students in a college, and so on. They can pray for healing when a member is sick.

For those who live alone, the family unit is a more extended grouping—the relatives and friends who live nearby, and those with whom we keep in close touch by letter or phone (the latter is a particularly useful means of praying with an individual in an emergency).

The prayers in Part 1 are written for such family situations and for occasions when individual members find themselves in hospital. They are very simple. They are printed first in this book because the Christian family is one of the best groupings within which we can begin to pray for healing for ourselves and for one another.

1 At home

Lord Jesus,
you shared the life of an earthly home at Nazareth
and visited the homes of your friends.
Come into our home
and touch those who are ill.
Restore them to health and wholeness
to the praise of your holy name.

2 For a sick child

Jesus, our Lord,
you became a child to save us.
Hold this child N. in your arms.
Give him your peace,
and make him better,
for your name's sake.

3 For the young

Thank you, Jesus,
for the young members of our family.
Heal in them any hidden memories
and unconscious fears
which they have received from us
through our inadequacies
as parents and older relatives.

May your Holy Spirit arm them
against the dangers and temptations of our society
which damage their health and ruin their relationships.
Protect them from evil influences,
and enable them to be lights of your truth and your love
among their friends
and those who come into contact with them.

So through them
may your Father and their Father be glorified.

4 For the healing of sick members

Almighty and ever-loving Father,
you bring health and salvation to all who believe in you.
Hear us as we ask for your loving help
for the sick in our family.
Send your Spirit that we may minister your healing to them.
Restore them so that together
we may follow Jesus your Son
as we minister to those around us.
And may our home be a refuge
where others may find his healing and strength,
because we have known your grace
and grown in your love.

5 During a long illness

Father, teach us to wait patiently
for the fulfilment of your will.
We look to you for love and grace,
that we may learn
to share in the sufferings of your beloved Son
and to receive his risen power.
Remove from our family anything
that bars the healing gifts of your Spirit.
We rejoice in your goodness to us,
in Jesus Christ.

6 Going into hospital

Jesus our Saviour,
make yourself known to me
as I enter the hospital.
Help me to adjust to this new manner of life.
Give me gratitude for those who care for me,
compassion for those in the ward with me,
and love for them all.

7 During medical treatment

Almighty God, eternal and compassionate,
giver of life and bringer of health,
grant that those who minister to me
in medical and nursing care
may be blessed in their work.
Enable me to cooperate with them
as we reach out for your healing.

As my weakness is banished
and my health is restored,
may I live by your Spirit
to glorify your holy name
through Jesus Christ.

8 Before an operation

Loving Father,
  I put myself into your hands.
Deliver me from fear of pain and of the unknown.
Set the cross of your dear Son over me,
  and guide with your wise Spirit
    the surgeon, the anaesthetist,
      and the theatre staff.
Anoint them as servants of your healing power,
  and while I am unconscious
    may my deepest thoughts and feelings rest
      in you.
May I sleep in your peace
  and awake to praise your mercy and your glory.

9 For hospital staffs

Father,
your Son Jesus Christ healed all kinds of sickness
as he went among the crowds
proclaiming the gospel of your kingdom.

Take all that is done in this hospital
in medical and nursing care,
in training and research,
in physiotherapy and psychiatry,
and in other practical ways,
and make it a continuation of his gracious ministry among us.

May the members of the staff,
whom you have equipped for this work,
come to know Jesus as their only Doctor and Saviour.
I ask this in his name.

10 At night in the ward

Lord, you have compassion on the sick
and you work by your Spirit through those who care for them.
Have mercy on all who cannot sleep tonight
because of their anxieties or their pain.
Bring them your healing comfort
to body, mind and spirit.

Be with those in charge of the wards,
with doctors and other members of the staff,
with those on duty in the casualty department,
in the ambulance stations, in the telephone exchange,
and elsewhere tonight.

I pray especially for those who are nervous
because they are inexperienced.
Equip them with all that is necessary
from your infinite wisdom and strength
to be agents of your grace, through Christ Jesus.

11 Sleeplessness

Be with me, merciful God,
as I lie awake through this long night.
May your Holy Spirit take my soreness
and bind me to your Son,
who suffered for my sins
and for those of the whole world.

May his healing and saving power
take away my discomfort
and establish me in his peace.
And may I rest in your love and righteousness,
knowing that in him I am your child.

Bring me, Father, the gift of sleep,
and may I wake in the morning refreshed
and renewed
because you have watched over me
and healed me as I slept.
Through Jesus I offer my prayer.

12 Discharged from hospital

My Lord and my God,
you are present everywhere.
Look down in your love
on the patients I am leaving here,
especially those I have met in the ward.

I thank you for the skill and care of the staff.
Renew them as they welcome the new patients
who are admitted today.
When I return home
help me to accept the changes as well as the joys.
Prepare me, my family and my friends
for our reunion.

Bind us together in the love of Jesus Christ,
and through the Holy Spirit
teach us to serve you
in our church and in our neighbourhood,
to your praise and glory.

13 For the disabled

Jesus, our Lord and Shepherd,
you had compassion on the weak and disabled,
the two blind beggars,
the crippled at Bethesda,
the deaf, the dumb,
the mentally ill,
and those troubled by evil spirits.

By the anointing of your Spirit
bring comfort, peace and healing
to N. in his distress.
May he have patience to accept what cannot
be changed
and faith to receive the healing which you
offer him
in body, mind and spirit.

Equip us with discernment and love
to encourage him to respond to you,
to the honour and glory of the heavenly Father.

14 For the elderly

All praise and glory are yours,
Lord our God,
for you have called us to serve you in love.

Thank you for the older members of our family.
Thank you for what they have done for us in the past,
and for what they do for us now
to point us to your future.

Bless N., who has served you many years,
and give him strength and courage
to continue to follow Jesus your Son.
We ask this through Christ our Lord.

15 For the dying

Father in heaven,
nothing can separate us from the love of Christ.
Whether we live or die, we are yours.
When we walk through the valley of the shadow of death
we fear no evil, for you are with us.

We come with N. beneath the cross of your beloved Son
and ask you to wash us in his blood.
In your mercy, forgive him and us our sins,
and prepare us to rejoice with your people in Zion,
where there is no mourning nor crying nor any more pain.
May your Holy Spirit, who raised Jesus from the dead,
raise N. and us to full healing and salvation to praise you in eternity.

16 For the bereaved

God of all mercy,
in your love for us you sent your Son
to break the bonds of sin and death
to invite us to share with him
the joy and glory of his resurrection.

Show your compassion on us
as we mourn the death of N.
Thank you for taking him from the darkness
of this world
into the glorious light of your kingdom.

Send us your Holy Spirit
and help us to surrender N. into your
Fatherly care.
Through the renewing grace of your Spirit
prepare us for the day when we are reunited
with our brothers and sisters in Christ
and every tear will be wiped away.

We ask this through Jesus our Lord.

17 Family thanksgiving for healing

Thanksgiving and praise be to you, our
heavenly Father
for the love you give us in so many different ways.

We thank you for one another:
other members of the family,
our friends and neighbours,
and the members of our church.

We thank you for teaching us how to be sorry for
our faults,
how to forgive, how to receive forgiveness
and how to minister your healing through
Jesus Christ
by the power of your gracious Spirit.

We thank you for the varied abilities and gifts
you have bestowed on us,
to share with one another
and to use for your purposes.

We thank you for difficult as well as happy times.
May our home be a little community where Jesus is
worshipped
and where your kingdom is honoured,
to your glory.

18 Family praise

Jesus, you invite your disciples
to call you their Friend.

We praise you that among our friends
you have revealed your love
in mending broken relationships,
in bestowing on them gifts of healing,
and in sharing among them your word.

May we be a company of those who follow your way
to the cross,
who receive the fulness of your Spirit,
and who are witnesses of your resurrection.

Send us, as the Father sent you, for the glory of
your name
and the extension of your kingdom.

Praise be to you, Lord Jesus, for ever.

PART 2

PERSONAL PRAYERS

Prayer is a movement of the Holy Spirit within us, urging us towards the Father through Jesus Christ. The words that we use are of secondary importance. Jesus warned his disciples that only pagans thought they would be heard because of their many words (Mt 6.7). Prayers are not more valid because they are polished, literary products. It is sincerity which matters: "You will seek me and find me when you seek me with all your heart" (Jer 29.31). In any case, God already knows our needs before we ask him (Mt 6.8).

Yet although words are secondary, they are still important. In everyday contacts with people, our words express our personalities, our feelings, our ideas, our attitudes and our hopes. Through the words we use, something of ourselves reaches out to others. We communicate with them.

And this is also true of the words we use when we pray. If we desire to offer ourselves to God, employing thoughtfully and sincerely the most appropriate words available to us, then the Holy Spirit will make those words a means of bringing us into communion with God. Indeed, he may well use them as a launch-pad from which to give us other words, inspiring us to pray with a faith and boldness beyond what we imagine possible.

Paul stressed the importance of "praying with the mind" as well as "praying with the spirit" (I Cor 14.15).

We should pray as we believe. Our understanding of the scriptures will influence what we say. So, too, will what we have learned from others—from the traditions of the past as well as the experiences of the present.

The words and forms used in public worship can feed our own prayers. This is a process which began with the first Christians, who used the scriptures and the set prayers of Judaism as models for their own devotions, developing the phraseology to express belief in God as Father, Son and Holy Spirit. We, too, can adapt the liturgical forms used in church for our own prayers (see the prefaces to Parts 4 and 5 as well as the Appendix.) The words of a prayer, then, can be a spiritual gift, manifesting Jesus Christ to ourselves and perhaps to others.

The twelve prayers in Part 2 are personal—in the first person singular ("I"). I have assumed that these are the sort which people use when they are alone. The prayers may be read aloud, but they are not intended for corporate use (these are in Part 3). Prayers like the one for inner healing (2.4) or the one offered in loneliness (2.8) are too personal to share with others.

Each prayer is introduced with a scriptural text, and the prayers themselves contain scriptural references. The first two prayers are for hope in God (2.1) and repentance of personal sins (2.2), vital for all healing; the next couple ask the Lord to enable us to accept the truth about himself and ourselves (2.3), leading on to inner healing (2.4—on this see also Part 8). Sometimes we need to offer our bodies to him for healing as well as our minds and spirits (2.5). At least once or twice in our lives (according to the law of averages) we shall be involved in an accident—in the home, in the car, while walking or travelling (2.6). Prayer does not always result in physical healing: it may mean that we have to persist patiently (2.7). Doctors, nurses and others are often involved in a ministry of healing (2.9 and 2.10), leading to greater wholeness (2.11), for which we can thank the Lord (2.12).

1 Hope

We have put our hope in the living God, who
is the Saviour of all men, and especially
of those who believe. 1 Tim 4.10

Father, your word tells us
that faith is being sure of what we hope for
and certain of what we do not see.

Fill me with a firm hope in your promises
and a living faith in your power.

Work your healing in me, living God,
that I may be whole
in body, mind and spirit,
to praise you and serve you
all my life.

I ask this through Jesus Christ,
your Son, my Saviour.

2 Repentance

Heal me, O Lord, and I shall be healed;
save me and I shall be saved,
for you are the one I praise. Jer 17.14

God of all glory and power,
you created me in your image,
and wonderfully re-created me
through the life, death, resurrection
and ascension of your Son.
Forgive my sins which separate me from you.
Stir my heart and mind to true repentance.

Renew in me the faith which comes from you.
And send your Holy Spirit upon me
that I may be healed,
and in his power joyfully praise you,
and serve you for the purposes of your kingdom.
I ask this in the name of Jesus Christ.

3 Truth

When he, the Spirit of truth, comes,
he will guide you into all truth. Jn 16.13

Spirit of God,
hold me so that I may continue in the word of the Son.
Then may I truly be his disciple;
and I will know the truth,
and the truth will make me free:
free of resentment and bitterness;
free of the fear of others
and of what they might think of me;
free of the shadows of past experiences,
of old and hurtful relationships;
free to ask for a gift of repentance,
that I might be forgiven
and healed.

Spirit of holiness,
work in me so that
in Christ I may become a new creation.
In him, the old has gone, the new has come,
for your work transforms us
making us more like him.

Spirit of truth,
reveal to me more and more
truth about myself.
Then I may be free to serve you,
with the Father and the Son.
and to honour your holy Name.

4 Inner healing

It is not the healthy who need a doctor, but the sick.
I have not come to call the righteous, but sinners.
Mk 2.17

Lord, I am crushed by this sense of my
unworthiness.
There is nothing in my life that I can call good.
I despise myself.
I loathe my thoughts and desires;
they poison and corrupt me.
If others could look into my heart
they would never want to know me again.

But you know me, Lord, intimately.
In your incarnate life
you saw into the hearts of women and men;
you discerned their secret faults.
There is nothing in me that is hidden from you.
Yet you still love me,
for you came to call sinners like me.
You are my Redeemer.

Lord, in your love, send cleansing fire into my
innermost being.
Drive from me the spirits of self-hatred and
depression,
banish them so that they never trouble me again.
And fill me with your Spirit
that I may grow in love for you and for others.

5 Body

While they were eating, Jesus took bread, gave thanks and broke it, and gave it to his disciples saying, "Take it; this is my body." Mk 14.22

Teach me, Lord God, to offer my body
as a living sacrifice to you:
my head, my arms, my legs;
my conscious and my deep unconscious—
impulses, thoughts, desires, ambitions—
all the known and unknown
that makes up the real me.

Teach me, also, to offer those parts of my body
which are sick and disabled.
Cleanse me, heal me, and renew me
by your Spirit.

Through the oblation of the body
of your beloved Son
may the offering of my body
be a spiritual act of worship,
holy and pleasing to you.

6 Accident

He will call upon me, and I will answer him:
I will be with him in trouble, I will deliver
him and honour him. Ps 91.15

I praise you, loving Father,
because your hand shielded me in this accident.
The awfulness of it –
the shock, the pain, the fear, the sense of
outrage—
overwhelmed me.
Yet in the midst of it I called upon you,
and you answered me.

I ask you in Jesus' name
to heal the others involved in it.
Help us forgive whoever was at fault.

And I ask you to guide me
through the consequences of this accident.
Heal my body,
deliver me from resentment,
and free me from emotional after-effects,
by the outpouring of your comforting Spirit.

7 Persistence

I waited patiently for the Lord;
he turned to me and heard my cry. Ps 40.1

Jesus, you taught your disciples,
always to pray and never to give up.
You know I am often tempted during this illness
to cease praying,
to give up hope,
and to sink into despair.

Give me the love and persistence
to cry out to the Father
day and night
knowing that through you
he hears me
and loves me.

8 Loneliness

If anyone loves me, he will obey my teaching. My Father will love him, and we will come and make our home with him. Jn 14.23

Creator of the universe,
Father of us all,
everything came into existence through your word.
You made the heavens, even the highest heavens,
and all their starry host.
Among the galaxies
this planet is but a speck of dust under your feet.

But my world lies within these four walls.
Beyond the window is a universe which becomes stranger every month, every year.
I shuffle from bed to chair,
from chair to table,
from table to toilet,
and then back to bed again.

Jesus, you are for ever united with our pained humanity.
Teach me by your Spirit to grow in faith
and to know your presence every day.
May my shuffles be my pilgrimage
as I seek your kingdom.

May my aches unite me with your cross.
And may I know the healing power of your
resurrection
and your glory here in my little space,
that my room may be your temple
where I can praise you always.

9 Medical care

The life I live in the body, I live by
faith in the Son of God, who loved me
and gave himself for me. Gal 2.20

Jesus, great Physician,
I have prayed for healing
and you have sent to me this doctor.
Supporting him are many who serve you
through medical skills, pharmacy,
and administrative and practical gifts.

Enable me to accept his service to me
as an agent of your healing power.
Guide him in his diagnosis
and grant that without fear or hesitation
I may cooperate with him
in his decisions and prescriptions.

And I pray that, through the treatment I receive,
you will heal me,
and bless the doctor
and those involved with him
in caring for me.

10 Carers

If anyone gives even a cup of cold water
to one of these little ones because he is
my disciple, I tell you the truth, he will
certainly not lose his reward. Mt 10.42

Heavenly Father, I praise you
for those you send to look after me.
They need patience to cope with my demands,
and compassion to accept me
when I am full of self-pity and complaints.

Help me through this illness to die to myself
each day,
and in your Spirit to be raised with Christ,
setting my heart on things above.
Grant me patience and compassion, too,
that I may serve them.
May our relationship grow in kindness and humility,
and may we be bound together in your love.

I thank you that, through their care,
you are giving me your healing
and renewing us in your Spirit,
for your honour and glory.

11 Wholeness

May the God of hope fill you with all joy
and peace as you trust in him, so that you
may overflow with hope by the power of
the Holy Spirit. Rom 15.13

Lord,
I come to you in penitence,
in trust, in hope:
I come praising your glorious name.

Heal every part of me, in body,
in mind, in spirit.
Save me from all evil.

For I long to serve you, in joy,
in peace and in power,
and to praise you all my days.

12 Give thanks

*Just as you received Christ Jesus as Lord,
continue to live in him, rooted and built
up in him, strengthened in the faith as you
were taught, and overflowing with
thankfulness.* Col 2.7

Father God,
the apostle urges me
to give thanks to you in all circumstances.
Through him you reveal
that this is your will for me
in Christ Jesus, your Son and my Saviour.

Surround me with your grace,
that as I have received him as my Lord,
I may continue to live in him,
and be rooted and built up in him.

Strengthen me in the faith in which I have
been taught
so that I may overflow with thankfulness
even in the midst of depression and sickness.

May your healing Holy Spirit lift me up
in praise and joy to sing,
Holy, holy, holy.

PART 3

CORPORATE PRAYERS

The prayers in Part 3 are corporate—in the first person plural ("we"). Although people may occasionally employ the first person singular when praying for healing in a group, it is more natural to use "we".

This form puts certain constraints on us when we pray. First, we have to remember that what we can say in prayer has to be said on behalf of the others as well as ourselves. We have to be sensitive to what the Holy Spirit may be saying through their hopes and ideas as well as our own. We cannot just talk to the Lord and keep silent before him as if there was no one else involved.

Second, the words we use are spoken aloud in such a way that the others can both follow the meaning of what we say and make our words their words, too. This is one of the reasons why certain Christians find it difficult to pray aloud spontaneously. It isn't because they don't know how to pray; it's because they're not confident they are sufficiently open to the Holy Spirit to be able to pray on behalf of others. For them it is probably better to begin by reading out set prayers, like those in this section, until they can create their own prayers freely.

Corporate prayer reflects the nature of the Christian community. Whenever we pray (even when we are praying alone), we do so as members of the church. "Where two or three come together in my name, there am I with them" (Mt 18.20). That is why Jesus taught his disciples to pray, "*Our* Father," not, "*My* Father." Through the Holy Spirit, our individual prayers are united with the prayer of Jesus Christ, who is our only intercessor with the Father in heaven (Heb 7.25).

These prayers are the kind of intercessions a group of Christians might offer as they prepare for and engage in the ministry of healing. They begin by submitting themselves to God's will (3.1) and by asking for forgiveness (3.2), faith (3.3) and guidance (3.4) before they seek the Holy Spirit's anointing (3.5) to undertake ministries of counselling (3.6), deliverance (3.7) or the laying on of hands for healing (3.8). Always they need to remember others who are engaged in this ministry (3.9). Their effectiveness will depend on their unity in the love of Jesus Christ (3.10). And when God's healing power is manifested to them, the Gospel is proclaimed (3.11), and those to whom they have ministered experience the life of Christ in greater abundance (3.12).

1 Preparation

I was shown mercy so that in me, the worst of sinners, Christ Jesus might display his unlimited patience as an example for those who would believe on him and receive eternal life.

1 Tim 1.16

Glorious and Holy God,
Everlasting Father,
you loved the world so much
that you gave your one and only Son,
that whoever believes in him shall not perish,
but have eternal life.

We surrender ourselves to you
so that in this ministry to those who are sick
we may be your messengers and servants,
united with your Messenger and Servant,
Jesus Christ.

In your great love you have called us
to serve you through them,
in their needs and hopes.
May we be rooted and established in that love
through the anointing of your Holy Spirit,
to love others as you love us.

2 Forgiveness

The Lord your God is with you,
he is mighty to save. Zeph 3.17

Holy Father,
in your love you sent your Son to be our Saviour.
He was pierced for our transgressions
and crushed for our iniquities.
Through his stripes we are healed.

Fill us with your Holy Spirit
that we may receive your healing
in body, mind and spirit.
We long to be a people who praise and serve you,
that others may turn to you
for forgiveness, healing and faith.

Grant this prayer, Father,
through your Son, our Redeemer.

3 Faith

Do not think of yourself more highly than you ought, but rather think of yourself with sober judgment, in accordance with the measure of faith God has given you. Rom 12.3

Lord God, you are the eternal Rock:
we trust in your word
that you will lead us in the path of righteousness.
You know our hesitations.
We cannot be sure of our own judgment
when we claim healing in your name.

Guard us from error,
protect us from the effects of our pride
and ambition,
and teach us to humble ourselves as little children.

Through the power of the cross
pour out the graces of forgiveness and renewal
on us and on those for whom we pray.
Heal them, Lord, by your Spirit,
that together we may praise you
and proclaim your love and greatness.
We ask this through your Son Jesus Christ.

4 Guidance

If anyone is thirsty, let him come to me and drink. Whoever believes in me, as the Scripture has said, streams of living water will flow from within him. Jn 7.37–38

Holy Spirit,
Comforter and Teacher of God's people,
guide us as we seek to minister your gifts of healing to those sick in mind and body whom you send to us.
Give us insights into their thoughts, their feelings, their lives, and their relationships.

Let the streams of your living water flow.
May they thirst for the love of Christ,
and in repentance and faith
drink the cup of salvation with hope and joy.

We ask this through him whom you sealed
as the Father's favoured One
at his baptism.

5 Anointed power

Now to him who is able to do immeasurably more than all we ask or imagine, according to his power that is at work within us, to him be glory in the church and in Christ Jesus throughout all generations, for ever and ever! Eph 3.20–21

God our Father,
you sent your Holy Spirit upon Jesus
at his baptism by John in the river Jordan,
announcing him as your Son.
He became the Christ, anointed to save us.

We pray that, through the same Spirit,
you will send your healing power
on your servant as we lay hands on him.

May the richness of your blessing flow over him,
and may the balm of your grace renew within him
everything that is broken and sore,
in mind and spirit as well as in body.

Your word reveals that you are able to do
immeasurably
more than we ask or imagine.
Let this healing bring glory to Christ Jesus
for we make this request in his name.

6 Counselling

You were once darkness, but now you are
light in the Lord. Eph 5.8

Almighty Father, eternal Wisdom,
the purposes of a man's heart are deep waters,
but a man of understanding draws them out.

Equip us with your wise Spirit
to serve our brother
as we minister to him.
Give us your discernment into the depths of
his heart.
Enable us in Jesus' name
to draw out from the memories of his past
whatever troubles him and makes him fearful.

Anoint him with your grace and healing
and bring him out of his darkness into your
glorious light,
so that as he looks back into former years
he may realise you were present with him then
as he knows your presence now.

7 Deliverance

Do not rejoice that the spirits submit to you, but rejoice that your names are written in heaven. Lk 10.20

Almighty God,
you sent your Son to rescue us from
unrighteousness,
and to give us the freedom
which only your sons and daughters can enjoy.
We pray for your servant troubled by evil powers.

In the name of Jesus Christ,
we claim the victory of the cross
over Satan and all his works.
Send the evil one into the place you have prepared
for him,
and fill your servant with the Holy Spirit,
that he may praise you and serve you
in righteousness for evermore.

8 Healing

Know this, you and all the people of Israel:
It is by the name of Jesus Christ of Nazareth,
whom you crucified but whom God raised from the dead, that this man stands before you healed. Ac 4.10

Merciful God,
all-loving and all-powerful,
Jesus taught that whatever we ask in his name,
we would receive.
Send healing gifts on your servant,
as we lay hands on him
that he may be cured of this illness.

May he glorify your Son
as his crucified Saviour
whom you raised from the dead as his Lord,
and may he follow him in your service
by the indwelling Spirit
all the days of his life.
We offer this prayer in Jesus' name.

9 Partnership

Holy brothers, who share in the heavenly calling, fix your thoughts on Jesus, the apostle and high priest whom we confess. Heb 3.1

Great Shepherd of the sheep,
Lord of the everlasting covenant
sealed in the blood of Jesus Christ,
the apostle and high priest whom we confess:

Your Spirit calls us into partnership with those
on whom you have poured many excellent gifts
for the healing of the sick,
the support of the disabled,
and the comfort of the dying.

Show us how to work with them,
even with those who do not acknowledge your holy name,
that together we may be servants of your healing love.

Grant that through sharing with us in ministry to others they may come to know you as their Father,
Jesus as their Saviour,
and the Holy Spirit as the source of their abilities.

10 Love one another

Lift up your eyes and look about you:
All assemble and come to you;
your sons come from afar, and
your daughters are carried on the arm. Isa 60.4

Lord Jesus, head of the church,
heal the divisions which separate us from
one another.
Send your Holy Spirit
to convict us of the guilt which is ours,
on our side of the separation.

Gather us together in your name
and increase our love for each other.
so that all men will know we are your disciples.

Then will your church become
a sign of healing in our neighbourhood,
and a witness to your kingdom
in your world.

11 Gospel

Praise be to the God and Father of our Lord Jesus Christ! In his great mercy he has given us new birth unto a living hope through the resurrection of Jesus Christ from the dead. 1 Pet 1.3

Almighty God, heavenly Father,
you have filled us with a living hope
through the resurrection of your Son.

Equip us with your Holy Spirit
to live the Gospel of your kingdom,
to proclaim your word, and to heal the sick.

We long that others may know you
and with us praise you
for your mercy and love.

We ask this in the name of him
who is the resurrection and the life,
Jesus Christ, our Lord.

12 Life

This is the testimony: God has given us
eternal life, and this life is in his Son. 1 Jn 5.11

Creator and Ruler of heaven and earth,
the universe is in the palm of your hand.

You sent your Son to give us life,
life in all its fulness
living water
bread eternal.

Enable us to live as you willed in the beginning,
washed in him,
fed by him,
that we may enter into that wholeness and salvation
which comes from you.

In your goodness, Lord, hear us.

PART 4

PRAYERS WITH RESPONSES

A litany is a form of prayer in which fixed responses are made by the congregation to short biddings or petitions said or sung by a leader (a priest, a deacon or cantors). The response, "We beseech thee to hear us, good Lord," is familiar to users of *The Book of Common Prayer*. It enables others in a group or a congregation to join in corporate prayer in what is virtually a form of choral speaking.

The repetition of an acclamation, a cry for mercy, or a verse, can help our minds to concentrate on the people for whom we are interceding by providing a rhythmic pattern within which our petitions are framed.

Part 4 contains four litanies. 4.1 addresses petitions in turn to the three Persons of the Trinity, and the responses are taken from Psalm 119. (The Psalms are a fruitful source for these kinds of responses.) It is personal in tone, and it concludes with a passage from Ephesians.

4.2 also has a response from the Psalms. This prayer is corporate and offers intercessions for all kinds of sick persons. It can be added to by others sharing in the prayers. Like traditional litanies, it ends with a brief collect.

In 4.3 the petitions are not addressed to God but to the people. The purpose of this form is to give individuals in the congregation or the group an opportunity to remember individuals with special needs whom they want to pray for and to offer intercessions silently while the leader pauses before saying, "Lord, in your mercy" (to which they reply, "Hear our prayer").

4.4 is addressed to the Second Person of the Trinity and employs the Jesus Prayer of the Orthodox tradition as its response.

1 Father, look on me in your love and mercy
as I wait for this operation (examination,
treatment, diagnosis).

Great peace have they who love your law,
and nothing can make them stumble. Ps 119.165

Jesus, stand by me with your understanding
and compassion
as I feel helpless and vulnerable.

Great peace have they who love your law,
and nothing can make them stumble.

Spirit, fill me with your hope and strength
as I need your presence and power.

Great peace have they who love your law,
and nothing can make them stumble.

Father, forgive the sins which have separated me
from you
and which have become part of my disease.

Let me live that I may praise you,
and may your laws sustain me. Ps 119.176

Jesus, set your cross between me and all that is evil
and bring me the joy of your salvation.

Let me live that I may praise you,
and may your laws sustain me.

Spirit, fill me with your healing grace
and complete in me your perfect will.

Let me live that I may praise you,
and may your laws sustain me.

Now to him who is able to do immeasurably more than all we ask or imagine, according to his power that is at work within us, to him be glory in the church and in Christ Jesus throughout all generations, for ever and ever. Amen. Eph 3.20–21.

2 Lord, we bring before you:
those who are suffering from physical and mental illnesses;
those dragged down by emotional and spiritual disorders.

They cried unto the Lord in their trouble:
He sent forth his word and healed them.
Ps 107.19–20

Those who are waiting for operations in hospitals, and those recovering from them;
those haunted with fears, or distressed in pain.

They cried unto the Lord in their trouble:
He sent forth his word and healed them.

Those who are confined to their homes or to institutions;
those who are disabled and dependent on the care of others.

They cried unto the Lord in their trouble:
He sent forth his word and healed them.

Those whose inner well-being has been damaged
through bad relationships
or evil experiences in the past;
those who can no longer reach out to you in faith
and hope.

They cried unto the Lord in their trouble:
He sent forth his word and healed them.

Those who are troubled by evil powers and impulses
beyond their control;
those trapped in addiction to alcohol, tobacco and
drugs.

They cried unto the Lord in their trouble:
He sent forth his word and healed them.

Stretch your hand over them, Lord.
Through Jesus Christ, send them healing and
salvation.
May your Holy Spirit bring them your love
and peace.

3 We gather in the name of Jesus Christ.
Let us pray for the work he has given us to do.

For the forgiveness of our sins,
our rejection of his will and our deafness to his call.

Lord, in your mercy,
hear our prayer.

For the protection of his Holy Spirit,
that we and those to whom we minister may be
shielded from all evil.

Lord, in your mercy,
hear our prayer.

For the gifts of compassion, discernment and faith,
that they may find his grace and healing through us.

Lord, in your mercy,
hear our prayer.

For the encouragement of a father and the
gentleness of a mother,
that they may know God as the love they long for.

Lord, in your mercy,
hear our prayer.

For the humility of Christ and the fire of the Spirit,
that to them we may be nothing and Jesus Christ
their all.

Lord, in your mercy,
hear our prayer.

For hope, joy and peace in our minds and hearts,
that they may be united with us in God's will.

Lord, in your mercy,
hear our prayer.

For the salvation and wholeness which comes from
the Lord,
that with one voice we may glorify him for ever.

Lord, in your mercy,
hear our prayer.

Almighty God, you know we long to see your healing and renewing strength in those for whom we pray. Pour your grace into them and into us, that we may fulfil your will through this ministry, and see the glory of your kingdom.

We ask this in the name of Jesus Christ our Lord.

4 Lord Jesus Christ,
gloriously risen and ever-reigning as our great high priest,
We ask you to intercede for us before the heavenly Father:

For those who are physically disabled in any way:
touch them as you touched the sick who were brought to you,
that your kingdom and compassion might be known.

Lord Jesus Christ, Son of the living God,
have mercy on us.

For those who are stained by sins
and who are rejected and despise themselves:
cleanse them and restore them,
that others will see in them your new creation.

Lord Jesus Christ, Son of the living God,
have mercy on us.

For those who suffer perpetual pain of mind and body:
draw them closer to yourself,
who suffered on the cross for us,
that they may share in your victory.

Lord Jesus Christ, Son of the living God,
have mercy on us.

For those who lock themselves behind the
doors of fear:
knock and enter into their lives,
that they will hear your words of peace.

Lord Jesus Christ, Son of the living God,
have mercy on us.

For those who are emotionally distressed
and unable to forgive themselves or to
forgive others:
change their hearts and heal their memories,
that they may enjoy your perfect freedom.

Lord Jesus Christ, Son of the living God,
have mercy on us.

For those who are dying
and who are afraid to commit themselves to your
loving care:
surround them with your love.
Make your presence known to them.

Lord Jesus Christ, Son of the living God,
have mercy on us.

Lord Jesus Christ, Son of the living God,
as our great high priest
you have gone through the heavens,
and yet remain with us by your Spirit.

We offer those intercessions in your name
to the heavenly Father.
In the compassion you showed to the sick,
the disabled and the dying,
reach out and touch those for whom we pray.
Speak the word that brings forgiveness, healing and peace.

And we praise you for the mercy you have shown us
and for the graces you will give us.
Glory be to you always!

PART 5

THANKSGIVINGS

There are many prayers of thanksgiving in the Bible. Some are in the psalms and in the prayers of the Old Testament. Others are in the New Testament, such as Jesus' prayer in Luke 10.21, and in passages of the apostolic letters.

A characteristic of these prayers is that God is "blessed." This sounds strange to English ears, as we are more familiar with the concept of God blessing his people (from our earliest memories of Christ's blessing of the children in Mark 10.16). But the other meaning—that we "bless" or thank God—is just as common in the scriptures.

The classic form of Jewish prayer is the *berakah*, or blessing. A typical example is the prayer of Abraham's servant when he had been successful in finding a wife for Isaac:

> Blessed be the Lord, the God of my master Abraham, who has not forsaken his steadfast love and his faithfulness towards my master. (Gen 24.27 RSV)

The apostolic church took over and adapted this prayer-pattern when they praised and thanked God, conscious that he had revealed himself to them in his Son Jesus Christ. So we find, for example,

> Blessed be the God and Father of our Lord Jesus Christ, who has blessed us in Christ with every spiritual blessing in the heavenly places (Eph 1.3 RSV)

That is a *berakah* that has been christianised (we might say "baptised") through its use within the church.

Prayers of thanksgiving are also affirmations of faith. We can only thank God if we have faith in him. Psalm 106 is but one example of a prayer which gives glory to God and then goes on to affirm the people's trust in him for what he will do for them ("Give thanks to the Lord for he is good; his love endures for ever"). Paul's letter to the Ephesians, which has just been quoted, begins with blessing God and continues with expressions of the apostle's confidence in what the Lord will do among those to whom he is writing.

Christian prayers of thanksgiving developed in various ways. Some prayers of thanksgiving are very simple, like 5.1. Others became recitals of gratitude for various gifts and graces from God. 5.2 is an example of how this kind of thanksgiving could be used by individuals in their private prayers.

The Psalms are a favourite source of prayers of praise, but since Part 6 is devoted to praying the psalms, I have turned to the Book of Revelation to illustrate in 5.3 how some texts in the New Testament can be woven into our thanksgivings.

Another important development was the evolution of the Christian-Jewish *berakah* into the prayer said over the bread and the wine at celebrations of the Lord's Supper. Jesus gave thanks over the bread and the wine on the night he was betrayed, and when the disciples followed his command to "Do this in remembrance of me," they almost certainly used—as he had done—the prayer of blessing which devout Jews used before meals at Passovertide.

This *berakah* was gradually extended to include thanksgiving for all that the Father had accomplished in the Son, and so it became the ancestor of the various families of eucharistic prayers in the church's liturgical tradition (see the prayer in the liturgy of anointing within the eucharist in Part 9). 5.4 is an example of how we can offer thanks to God by borrowing the shape and the phraseology of the beginning of a modern eucharistic prayer up to and including the *Sanctus*.

1 Thank you for creating us
Thank you for saving us
Thank you for healing us
  Father Almighty

Praise you for dying for us
Praise you for rising for us
Praise you for being with us
  Lord Jesus Christ

Bless you for cleansing us
Bless you for renewing us
Bless you for strengthening us
  Holy Spirit of God

2 Thank you, Father,
that when I called, you answered me,
and when I was in trouble, you delivered me.

You upheld me through the suffering and the uncertainty.
Though I hardly remembered you
in the midst of that crisis,
you did not forget me.
I thank you through Jesus Christ
for the salvation you give me through him,
your love and mercy,
your strength and guidance,
your presence night and day.

I thank you for your Holy Spirit
who brings me your comfort and healing.
through the prayers and concern
of my sisters and brothers in Christ.

I thank you for the skills he brings
to medical and nursing staff,
to those who research and administer,
who clean and carry,
who serve me in many practical ways.

I thank you, Father, for all the love and grace
you have shown me through this illness.
I praise you that it will be for me
a step on my pilgrimage as I follow you.

Glory be to the Father, and to the Son,
and to the Holy Spirit:
as it was in the beginning, is now,
and shall be for ever.

3 *You are worthy, our Lord and God,*
to receive glory and honour and power,
for you created all things,
and by your will they were created
and have their being. (Rev 4.11)

You made us:
in the midst of this wonderful creation
you brought us into being.

Life is your gift, Lord.
We are humbled that you should have handed it to us:
we, your creatures,
made for your glory and honour,
sharers in your power.

Praise and thanksgiving be to you for ever,
God our Creator.

Salvation belongs to our God,
who sits on the throne,
and to the Lamb. (Rev 7.10)

We turned away from you, Lord,
from light to darkness
from wholeness to sickness,
from obedience to sin,
from life to death.

We, your creatures, rejected your gift.
But you sent your Son as our Redeemer,
the Lamb, who with his blood,
purchased our salvation and healing.

In him we are made new,
restored,
amazingly healed.

Praise and thanksgiving be to you for ever,
God our Saviour.

Worthy is the Lamb, who was slain,
to receive power and wealth
and wisdom and strength
and honour and glory and praise. (Rev 5.12)

Through your Son we receive your Spirit,
your power and wisdom,
to honour and praise and glorify your name.

In him we are invited
to the foretaste of your heavenly banquet.
We bow before you in adoration and love.

Praise and thanksgiving be to you for ever,
God our Strength.

To him who sits on the throne and to the Lamb
be praise and honour and glory and power,
for ever and ever. (Rev 5.13)

4 All holy and glorious Father, our Creator God,
we give you thanks and praise
because in your loving wisdom
you brought all things into being.

Again and again we have turned away from you;
yet in every age your steadfast love has called us to return
and to live in union with you:
for it is your eternal purpose
to offer us new life and healing
and to make us holy.
We give you thanks and praise
because through your Son, Jesus Christ,
who took our nature upon him,
you have redeemed the world from the bondage of sin.

He accepted baptism and consecration as your Servant
to announce the good news to the poor,
to cast out demons, and to heal the sick.
He offered himself on the cross
as a sacrifice for sin
that we might be washed clean by his blood.
You raised him from the dead by the power of your Spirit
and exalted him to your right hand
to reign with you as our King for ever.

We give you thanks and praise
because Christ gives us the royal priesthood
and, loving us as his sisters and brothers,
invites us to share in his ministry,
proclaiming the Gospel of your kingdom
and announcing forgiveness of sins, victory over evil,
and healing of illnesses in his name.

We give you thanks and praise
because through Christ you fill us with your Spirit,
and gather us to become a people for yourself,
to make known in every place the perfect offering which he made for the glory of your name.

Through him you equip us with natural and spiritual gifts to care for those who suffer distress, disease and disablement
in body, mind and spirit.
You reveal the signs of your kingdom
in healings and liberations,
in prayers and sacraments,
in medical care and nursing skill,
and above all in love of one for another.

Therefore with angels and archangels
and with all the company of heaven,
we proclaim your great and glorious name,
for ever praising you and saying:

Holy, holy, holy Lord,
God of power and might,
heaven and earth are full of your glory.
Hosanna in the highest.

Blessed is he who comes in the name of the Lord.
Hosanna in the highest.

PART 6

PRAYING THE PSALMS

The Psalter is the hymn book of ancient Israel, compiled from older collections of songs for use in the temple of Zerubbabel (Ezra 5.2; Hag 1.14). The Hebrew title for it is "Book of Praises." Although not all psalms are praises, it is a fitting name, for in the Psalter the theme of praise and thanksgiving recurs again and again.

The songs in the first half of the Psalter were anciently ascribed to David. Although this tradition has long been questioned by Old Testament scholars, it is possible some of the earliest songs—or, at any rate, parts of them—go back to David's reign, if not to the king himself. The rest were written over the next five hundred years or so.

Most commentators classify the psalms according to the occasions on which particular songs may have been used—enthronement psalms for royal occasions, choruses of trust in God, national hymns of thanksgiving, penitential liturgies, and so on. Some are associated with the worship of Israel during the festivals—Passover, the feast of Weeks and the feast of Tabernacles.

But many of the psalms are of a personal nature. We recognise in them the questionings and the agonisings of individuals who sought to understand God's will for them amid the often perplexing and sometimes terrifying situations in which they found themselves. What they said strikes a universal note, and so their songs still speak to us and for us today.

The early Christians did not doubt that in the psalms, as elsewhere in the Old Testament, they heard the voice of the Lord. So, for example, the author of Hebrews, explaining how followers of Christ are made members of God's family, quoted Psalm 22.22 when he wrote:

> Jesus is not ashamed to call them brothers. He says, "I will declare your name to my brothers, in the presence of the congregation I will sing your praises." Heb 2.12

The Psalter continued to be used by those Jews who, as disciples of Jesus Christ, became members of the apostolic church (e.g., Acts 4.25–26), and so also by the wider Christian community drawn together by those who were baptised in the Gentile world. Its contents were interpreted in the light of the Gospel, and its songs were adapted for Christian beliefs and practices.

For us the psalms have a profound significance, since the Gospel proclaimed by Jesus and taught by the apostles reveals to us much more than the psalmists ever knew about the infinite quality of God's love, the gravity of sin, and the glory promised to the faithful disciples of Christ. The hopes which once echoed in their prayers and songs have been fulfilled: the Messiah has come, he now reigns, and all nations are summoned to praise him.

In Christian liturgical and devotional traditions certain concepts in the psalms are allegorised: "Israel" becomes the church, "enemies" evil temptations and spiritual foes, "the law" the whole purpose of God as revealed through Jesus Christ, "the covenant" the new covenant won through the cross, "Jerusalem" the kingdom of God, and so on. When we use the psalms for our prayers we instinctively employ the same allegories; but the Holy Spirit may lead us in different ways as we use the texts for our confessions and petitions, thanksgivings and praises.

I have written a few examples of how some psalms might be used in prayer for healing. 6.1 selects verses of Psalm 139 in a meditation on the healing of our bodies and our hope of the resurrection. We read a verse at a time and let our own thoughts and prayers develop from it.

6.2 uses verses of Psalm 38 as a basis for reflection on inner healing.

In 6.3 a selection of verses from Psalm 77 inspire in us a prayer which begins with doubting whether God hears us but then goes on to renew our faith as we remember (as the psalmist did) God's goodness to us in the past. This is followed by three verses from Psalm 86 which express our willingness to await a new manifestation of God's goodness in the midst of present illness.

Verses of Psalm 91 become the steps for a prayer of faith in God in 6.4.

6.5 is different. In this example the verses of Psalm 121 have been freely re-written as a prayer for healing.

1 Created by God

You created my inmost being;
you knit me together in my mother's womb.

Everything about me was planned and made by
you, Lord.
The chromosomes from my father and mother
came together in a pattern
that determined what I would be like;
and those characteristics were laid down
through my grandparents and my ancestors,
through the generations of our families
in ages long ago.

I praise you because I am fearfully and wonderfully made;
your works are wonderful,
I know that full well.

And you created me for your praise, Lord God,
that your glory should be reflected
in me as a person,
redeemed through the cross of your Son,
and re-created by the power of your Spirit.
Even my body, though it is ageing and often sick,
can still be transfigured
when I surrender myself to you.

My frame was not hidden from you
when I was made in the secret place.
When I was woven together in the depths of the earth,
your eyes saw my unformed body.

I am part of the universe, of this planet,
with all its joys and pains,
its beauties and horrors.
The earth is my foster-mother;
part of me belongs to her dust.
So does my sickness.
But another part of me belongs to you, my God,
for in your great love and mercy
you have called me to be your child.
You are my true Father and Mother.

All the days ordained for me
were written in your book
before one of them came to be.

This dust which is my body
you have given an eternal destiny
in the resurrection
and consummation of all things in Jesus Christ.

Lord, I want to trust you more.
Give me grace which enables me
to rest in your promises,
and to set aside the barriers of sin and unbelief
which prevent me from receiving your healing.

Re-create those deep levels of my consciousness
where the past has left its wounds,
its prejudices, and its disobediences.
Renew me in your love,
that my love for you and for my friends
may be that of one who is born of you
and knows you.

Search me, O God, and know my heart;
test me and know my anxious thoughts.
See if there is any offensive way in me,
and lead me in the way everlasting.

Ps 139.13–16, 23–24.

2 Come quickly

O Lord, do not rebuke me in your anger
or discipline me in your wrath.
For your arrows have pierced me,
and your hand has come down upon me.
Because of your wrath there is no health in my body;
my bones have no soundness because of my sin.
My guilt has overwhelmed me
like a burden too heavy to bear.

I do not know, Lord, how far my own faults
have made me as I am.
I can think of sins which I have committed,
and for them I am truly sorry.
Forgive me also for those sins I cannot recognise
through my blindness to your will.
Use this sickness to enlighten me,
show me how I have offended your word,
and restore me in your peace.

All my longings lie open before you, O Lord:
my sighing is not hidden from you.
My heart pounds, my strength fails me;
even the light has gone from my eyes.

And when you enlighten me, Lord,
heal me of this illness.
Through Jesus Christ I ask you
to touch me with your right hand
and to speak the word that brings healing and wholeness.

I wait for you, O Lord;
you will answer, O Lord my God.

O Lord, do not forsake me:
be not far from me, O my God.
Come quickly to help me,
O Lord my Saviour.

Ps 38.1–4, 9–10, 15, 21–22.

3 Lord, answer me

I cried to God for help;
I cried out to God to hear me.
When I was in distress, I sought the Lord;
at night I stretched out untiring hands
and my soul refused to be comforted.
I remembered you, O God, and I groaned;
I mused, and my spirit grew faint.

Lord, you seemed so far from me.
I prayed, but it was like talking to myself.
I had no sense of your presence.
I wondered if my faith had been an illusion,
a wish fulfilled only in my imagination.
For my healing was delayed.
The illness went on and on.
The depression crushed me.
There was no answer to my petitions
for others or for myself.

Then I thought, "To this I will appeal:
the years of the right hand of the Most High."
I will remember the deeds of the Lord;
yes, I will remember your miracles of long ago.
I will meditate on all your works
and consider all your mighty deeds.

Yet, when I look back,
I can recognise how often you showed your love for me:
through relatives and friends you spoke to me and cared for me;
through members of your church you encouraged me and guided me.

I have discerned your leading in the choices I made,
and I remember many occasions
when you shielded me from evil.
I have known moments of silence and awe
when I was aware of your voice within me.

Lord, your goodness has been manifested to me
over all the years of my life.
How can I doubt your presence now?

Your ways, O God, are holy,
What god is so great as our God?
You are the God who performs miracles;
you display your power among the peoples.
With your mighty arm you redeemed your people,
the descendants of Jacob and Joseph.

Lord, I am content to await your will.
If it be healing, then let me be healed.
If I have to suffer this illness for a time yet,
then grant me willing submission to your
purposes through it.

Bring joy to your servant,
for to you, O Lord,
I lift up my soul.

You are forgiving and good, O Lord,
abounding in love to all who call to you.
Hear my prayer, O Lord,
listen to my cry for mercy.
In the day of my trouble I will call to you,
for you will answer me.

Ps 77.1–3, 10–12, 13–15; 86.4–7.

4 His shelter

He who dwells in the shelter of the Most High
will rest in the shadow of the Almighty.

Lord, within your church
I am resting in your shadow.
Around me are those who have been baptised
in water and in the Spirit;
they, too, are dwelling in your shelter.
We are your body.

I will say to the Lord, "He is my refuge and my fortress,
my God, in whom I trust."

You protect me in all things.
I flee to you for safety.
In your arms I find security and strength.
I trust you, Jesus:
uphold me when my faith is tested.

"Because he loves me," says the Lord, "I will rescue him;
I will protect him, for he acknowledges my name."

Lord, I place myself into your care:
every part of me –
body, mind and spirit –
I hand over to you,
my refuge and my fortress.

"He will call upon me, and I will answer him;
I will be with him in trouble,
I will deliver him and honour him."

Thank you, merciful Lord, for that promise.
  I can face anything knowing that you are with me.
Already you have delivered me
  and brought me to great honour
    by saving me and bringing me
  into the family of your heavenly Father.
How great is your love for us
  that we should be called children of God!

"With long life will I satisfy him
and show him my salvation."

Glory to the Father, and to the Son,
  and to the Holy Spirit,
    now and for ever. Ps 91.1–2, 14–16.

5 Psalm 121

We will lift up our eyes to the hills—
where does our healing come from?
Our healing comes from the Lord,
the Maker of heaven and earth.

He will not allow our illnesses to overwhelm us—
he who watches over us does not forget us;
indeed, he who watches over the whole church
loves and saves us.

The Lord watches over us –
the Lord is our shade at our right hand;
the sickness will not crush us in despair by
day nor will its effects take away our inner peace
by night.

The Lord will bring us his salvation—
he will heal our lives completely;
the Lord will watch over our coming and going
both now and for evermore.

PART 7

PRAYING WITH THE SCRIPTURES

Praying for healing is essentially a matter of seeking God's will and believing that he wants to use us in fulfilling it. To ask anything in Jesus' name is to pray as he did: "Not my will but yours be done" (Lk 22.42). Or, as he said to his disciples, "I do nothing on my own but speak just what the Father has taught me" (Jn 8.28).

Since the Bible is our primary source for learning God's will, it is also our primary source for prayer. The more we read and reflect on the scriptures, the more we open ourselves to the word of God, for as we think about the texts, the Holy Spirit moves within us to witness to the truth revealed through them.

This devotional use of the Bible is known as "meditation" or "mental prayer." Traditional Christian teaching distinguishes "mental prayer" from "vocal prayer" on the grounds that, when we meditate, our voices are usually silent. The distinction is not entirely accurate, for even when we pray aloud presumably our minds are active, too!

Meditation is not the same as Bible study. When we *study* the scriptures, we approach them as the product of a certain people of a certain period in human history. Then we seek to understand them by setting passages beside one another, seeing them within the Bible as a whole, and learning what interpretations have been given them over the centuries by the church. But when we *meditate* on the Bible, we read a passage in the faith and hope that the Spirit will use it as a means through which we shall hear what God is saying to us now.

Often by the end of a meditation, or shortly afterwards, we shall be conscious of a new insight into his will—perhaps a fresh slant on something that has been bothering us, or guidance on a choice we have to make. Nearly always we shall be conscious that we have encountered God in some way through our meditation, even when our thoughts have been haphazard and distracted.

True, the distinction between Bible study and meditation is never clear–cut. In practice we shall find ourselves slipping from one to the other. Bible study becomes meditation when we use it to seek the illumination of God's word; and, when we are trying to meditate on a passage of scripture, it is easy to be carried away by the interesting details in the footnotes and to forget we are supposed to be praying (I had to give up using my annotated Bible in meditation for that reason!).

We do not have to be competent Bible students before we can meditate on the scriptures. Mental prayer does not depend on our intellectual ability. It depends on our willingness to read the Bible and to make opportunities to reflect on what we read. One of the wonderful things about the scriptures is that, whoever we are, the Spirit can reveal the Lord to us through them. When Simon Peter confessed that Jesus was the Christ, the Son of the living God, the Lord said, "Blessed are you, Simon son of Jonah, for this was not revealed to you by man, but by my Father in heaven" (Mt 16.17).

When we settle down to meditate on a passage of scripture, then, we do not ignore what we know of it through biblical studies, but we do not stay at that level.

We use the information such studies give us to help us understand what has been written and go on to ponder over the passage, allowing the Spirit to direct our thoughts and imaginations as we savour key words, themes, outstanding verses, pictures conjured up in our minds, and so on.

Finally we offer to God a prayer based on the passage and on our reflections about it. Again, the Spirit will teach us how to pray, if we wait for him. That prayer is part of our response to what God is saying to us through the Bible. The rest of our response is what we do in practical obedience to his word.

I should add that practically everybody finds meditation a testing kind of prayer. When we attempt to meditate we often seem to spend much of the time struggling with distractions and wandering thoughts. But experience shows that it is in trying to pray that God meets us inwardly; he doesn't wait until we're meditating with our mental and emotional processes operating perfectly before he approaches us!

Certainly meditation is doubly difficult when we are ill. In those circumstances, the most that we can manage are a few arrow prayers during the day and an occasional intercession in the night (especially if we're in hospital, see 1.10). But if we have attempted to meditate regularly while we have been healthy, we shall have built up in our memories a store of biblical material which will be useful on days when we are not well enough to read our Bibles and pray systematically. We shall find ourselves remembering texts through which the Lord will speak comfortingly to us and with which we can form brief prayers in response to him.

In this section I have attempted to demonstrate four different ways of making a meditation on scriptural passages.

7.1 is a straightforward meditation which begins with noting the sort of things about the passage which we might pick up from any Bible study on it. This I have called the commentary. It continues with the reflections —the ideas that might come into our minds as we consider the passage for several minutes. Then our thoughts move into prayers of penitence, intercession and thanksgiving as we take what we have read and seek to respond to God through it.

In 7.2 the meditation follows a form which is intended to help us to exercise our imaginations more. This particular form is given various names. I have always known it as "the five Ps"—the initials of the five stages of the meditation (prepare, picture, ponder, pray, promise). In the preparation we familiarise ourselves with the passage, drawing on the results of Bible study, and ask the Lord to help us hear him through what we read (for this prayer I have used the collect for the Second Sunday in Advent in the Church of England's ASB). Then we move on to picture the scene, imagining what it would have been like if we had been present. Ponder and pray are the same as reflection and prayer in 7.1. Promise means we undertake to do something practical as a result of our meditation.

In 7.3 these same elements are interwoven into a reading of the passage without attempting to keep to a set pattern. We read through the verses slowly, pausing to think about them, perhaps to ask questions about them, and praying about them, and then moving on.

7.4 is more discursive—the sort of meditation which is suitable when we read passages from the epistles where there is little to exercise our imaginations.

A meditation is a highly personalised kind of prayer.

No two people will reflect on a scriptural passage in exactly the same way, and their response will differ according to their spirituality and their circumstances. There is, then, something artificial about the meditations I have written here. I will simply repeat that they are only intended to be examples to help you get started. Eventually you will discover your own patterns of meditation. If you persist with this kind of prayer, it will help you to think *biblically* about situations in your life—especially, in this case, your participation in the ministry of prayer for healing, either as an intercessor or as a patient.

1 Mark 2.1–12 Jesus heals the paralytic

Commentary

The scene was one of the common dwelling-places, which had an outside staircase to a flat roof made with wood and clay that could easily be removed and repaired. Inside, Jesus was addressing a crowd which was so large that it overflowed outside the doorway. When the four men carrying the paralysed man on a stretcher found they could not get in, they took the patient up on to the roof, made an opening, and lowered him in.

Coming near the beginning of the gospel, the story reveals Jesus as the bringer of God's forgiveness. By healing the man of his paralysis, Jesus demonstrated his divine authority. The ancient world was well aware of the mysterious connection between sickness and sin (in ways that modern psychosomatic medicine has sometimes vindicated), and the evangelist saw the particular disease from which the man on the stretcher was suffering as a sign of the paralysing effect of sin.

From the viewpoint of Mark and his readers, it was

not surprising that Jesus commenced his ministry to the paralytic by absolving him. They believed the Messiah, the Anointed One of God—the One who was crucified and who rose again for the remission of sins—had authority to do that. But the Jewish teachers of the law did not recognise such authority in Jesus. Nor did they expect the Messiah to forgive sins when he came. That was the prerogative of God alone. The most a man could do in this life, they thought, was to plead to God for forgiveness in his prayers, adopt the signs of penitence (ashes, sackcloth, fasting), and offer the appropriate sacrifices for ritual cleansing, especially by joining in the ceremonies of the Day of Atonement. Divine forgiveness would then be manifested in the blessings which God gave the penitent.

Jesus, having pronounced the absolution, went on to exercise his authority by healing the paralysed man, claiming for himself the title of Son of Man—a Messianic title. The result was that the crowd were amazed and praised God—the reaction of awe and wonder at the mighty work of God.

Reflections

(1) *Jesus saw their faith*—the faith of the four friends, or the faith of the four plus that of the paralytic? We know that Jesus healed those who relied on the faith of others (see Luke 7.1–10, the healing of the centurion's servant). We are interdependent under God, relying so much on the prayers of our friends. Do we pray for others as we hope that they pray for us?

(2) Superficially it might have looked as if Jesus was offering a stone when the four friends expected bread—saying their friend was forgiven when they had hoped

Christ would cure him of his dreadful affliction. But Jesus discerned the origin of the man's sickness in his past life. That had to be dealt with first, otherwise there could be no real healing. How many people would walk out of surgeries and mental hospitals today if they knew that Jesus bears our guilt and wipes out our past? How far are the sicknesses and disorders of life due to our inability to seek forgiveness from God and from those we have offended?

(3) The Gospel of the kingdom of God does not offer us all healing when we turn to Jesus or when we pray in faith for the healing of others. Complete healing belongs to the fulfilment of that kingdom at the end of the ages. "He will wipe every tear from their eyes. There will be no more death or mourning or crying or pain, for the old order of things has passed away" (Revelation 21.4). But the Gospel does offer us all God's forgiveness through Jesus Christ. That is the healing we can begin to enjoy now, if we confess our sins and turn to the cross of Jesus in faith.

(4) The Gospel, then, is about the grace of God which wipes out past sins and overshadows us with his Spirit to enable us to fight against temptation now and in the future. We are equipped for this spiritual battle. It may also be, for some, signified in mental and physical renewal, including healing. But that is secondary: "I consider that our present sufferings are not worth comparing with the glory that will be revealed in us" (Romans 8.18).

Prayer

Thank you, Lord, for my friends,
who carry me by their prayers
into your presence.
Bless them for their faithfulness to you
and their care for me.
May I never weary of my ministry of intercession
for them,
for those in need,
for those who do not know how to seek your
salvation.

I wish to repent of my sins,
especially. . .
For these,
and for all other sins which I cannot remember,
I am truly sorry,
I resolve not to sin again,
and I ask of you, my Redeemer,
the forgiveness which you have won for me
through your cross.

Take away everything that paralyses me
and prevents me walking in your ways:
evil thoughts,
sinful impulses,
depressions and anxieties,
tensions within myself
and between me and others.

Send your Holy Spirit
that I may be freed from them for ever,
and glorify your Name.

2 Luke 17.11–19 The ten lepers

Prepare

The Hebrew word for leprosy is derived from a primary root which means "stricken of God." The strict laws relating to it in Judaism seem to have had a religious or spiritual reason behind them as well as a sanitary one. The word was used to describe a variety of skin diseases as well as the modern *mycobacterium leprae* (or whatever its form was in the ancient world).

Lepers were separated from society because they were regarded as ritually unclean; behind this was also a suspicion that they had offended God to the extent that he had punished them with this affliction. In the Old Testament there are three examples of individuals being smitten with skin diseases as a punishment for sin—Miriam, Gehazi and Uzziah (Num 12.2; 2 Kg 5 and 2 Chron 26).

The elaborate regulations for the cleansing of a leper are prescribed in Leviticus 14. They include an inspection of the leper by a priest, a sacrificial offering of two birds, sprinklings with hyssop, seven days' quarantine with shavings and washings, and a further sacrificial offering of a male lamb on the eighth day. By the time of Christ, the healing of leprosy was expected as one of the signs of the messianic age (Lk 7.22).

The border between Samaria and Galilee was well away from the centre of Judaism. Galilee had a high proportion of Gentiles among its population, which accounts for the contempt which strict Jews had for the region (e.g. "You will find that a prophet does not come out of Galilee" — Jn 7.52). The Samaritans claimed to be the descendants of the northern kingdom of Israel, but they were considered to be schismatics by the

Judaeans, who feared and hated them.

Blessed Lord,
who caused all holy Scriptures
to be written for our learning:
help us to hear them,
to read, mark, learn, and inwardly digest them
that, through patience, and the comfort
of your holy word,
we may embrace and for ever hold fast
the hope of everlasting life,
which you have given us in our Saviour Jesus Christ.

Picture

We imagine Jesus and his disciples striding along the road towards the village, with the hills of Lower Galilee to the north and Mount Carmel over in the west near the coast. It was the road that pilgrims to Jerusalem took—sometimes at the risk of their lives.

The ten men appear on the side of the road on the outskirts of the village. The horrible effects of the disease are only too apparent. Blotched skin, twisted limbs, disfigured faces. In accordance with the law their clothes were torn and their hair hung loose (Lev 13.45).

If we had been one of the disciples, we would have felt repulsed. What sins had these wretches committed to be suffering such awful punishment? What had they done that had caused God to be so angry with them?

As they get closer we feel a slight alarm. They should be keeping their distance and crying out, "Unclean! Unclean!" If they touched us, we would be ritually unclean, too. But to our surprise they shout something else: "Jesus, Master, have pity on us!" Through the pain and despair of these ten miserable men we detect in that cry a note of hope.

We sense a surge of pity in the Master as he pauses to look at them.

"Go, show yourselves to the priests."

We watch them slowly turn away, half-amazed, half-disappointed, looking at one another, and occasionally glancing back at Jesus.

They disappear into the village. We are about to continue on our way, when suddenly we see one of them running back. His hands are waving joyfully in the air, he is laughing and crying, and as he draws near we see that his face is perfectly clear of the disease.

He rushes up to Jesus, drops on his knees, and stammers his thanks.

Jesus puts his hand on his head.

"Were not all ten cleansed?" he asks, with a hint of reproach in his voicc. "Where are the other nine?"

He turns to us.

"Was no one found to return and give praise to God except this foreigner?"

Foreigner? we wonder. We look at the man. Of course, a Samaritan! Who would have believed a Samaritan would kneel to a Jew? Only when that Jew was instrumental in healing him. Only when that Jew demonstrated he was truly the Son of God.

"Rise and go," says Jesus to the kneeling man. "Your faith has made you well."

The man stands up, and with a final word of thanks he marches off towards the village like a new man. We hear him singing praises to God as he goes. It does not occur to us to ask the Master if by "made you well" he meant that the man had been forgiven his sins as well as healed of his disease. In our (Jewish) understanding the two blessings are one.

Ponder

Leprosy is a vivid demonstration of the effects of sin in our lives. The one who was excluded from the community was regarded as already dead. When Miriam was inflicted with leprosy she was treated "like a stillborn infant coming from its mother's womb with its flesh half eaten away" (Num 12.12). The disease affects the human body as sin affects the human soul. Sin separates us from God and from one another; it ruins what God created as perfect and in his own image; it begins within us and is not always recognised at first; it rots away human life, paralysing us and taking away our sensitivity; it disfigures and distorts both us and our attitudes; it results in death. An unrepentant sinner is a spiritual leper.

Jesus "heals" us in the fullest sense of that word—forgives us of sin as well as cures us of sickness. We believe it is his will that we should be healed and that his healing is physical, mental and emotional as well as spiritual. The faith which saves is faith in him, not faith in the quality of our expectations! What must I confess to him before I am cleansed? Do I need to talk to someone—my pastor—about my sins and ask him to pray for my forgiveness as well? Is this how I should "show myself to the priest"?

It was for my healing that Christ died for me. There is an old tradition that Jesus was leprous when he hung on the cross. This stems from the word used in Isaiah 53.4, where the suffering servant is described as "stricken by God"—its roots are the same as those for "leprosy" in Hebrew.

Pray

Have mercy on me, O God, according to your
unfailing love;
according to your great compassion blot out
my transgressions.
Wash away all my iniquity and cleanse me from
my sin.

(Ps 51.1–2)

Father eternal, giver of light and grace,
we have sinned against you and against
our fellow men,
in what we have thought,
in what we have said and done
through ignorance, through weakness,
through our own deliberate fault,
We have wounded your love,
and marred your image in us.
We are sorry and ashamed,
and repent of all our sins.
For the sake of Jesus Christ who died for us,
forgive us all that is past;
and lead us out from darkness
to walk as children of light.

Cleanse me with hyssop, and I shall be clean;
wash me, and I shall be whiter than snow.

(Ps 51.7)

Promise

Father in heaven,
enlighten me with your Holy Spirit,
that I may discern the sins
which mar your image like leprosy in me
give me the grace of humility
to repent and confess my faults
that I may be cleansed through the sacrifice of your Son,
Jesus Christ, my Saviour and Lord.

3 Acts 16.25–34 The apostles and the jailer

About midnight Paul and Silas were praying and singing hymns to God, and the other prisoners were listening.

With Silas, Paul had been stripped and flogged before being thrown into prison. In his letters he referred to the ill-treatment he received at Philippi (Phil 1.30 and 1 Th 2.2). Yet he could still praise God. He had written, "Be joyful always; pray continually; give thanks in all circumstances, for this is God's will for you in Christ Jesus" (1 Th 5.16–17).

Other Christians have followed the apostles' example. One of the stories told of Maximilian Kohbe in Auschwitz was that he led his companions in the death cell in prayer. Some, who have been held in prison under oppressive regimes, have testified that during that time they wonderfully experienced the presence of Christ.

Lord, how easily we convince ourselves that we are praising you by singing tuneful hymns and choruses! Maybe we would learn the reality of praise if we were persecuted for being your disciples.

What did the other prisoners think of the apostles' prayers and songs? Were they merely curious, or scornful, or even envious? Or had they heard of the Gospel Paul and Silas had proclaimed in Philippi and of the conversion of Lydia and her household?

Suddenly there was such a violent earthquake that the foundations of the prison were shaken. At once all the prison doors flew open, and everybody's chains came loose.

That was a remarkable answer to prayer! Usually we associate earthquakes with disasters. But here was a tremor that burst open the barred gates. If only all our prayers had such striking results!

There had been another shaking of the foundations earlier, when Peter and John had been released by the Sanhedrin. The apostolic church in Jerusalem had praised God, and the place where they were meeting was rocked when the Holy Spirit came upon them. They were enabled to speak the word of God boldly (Ac 4.31).

Spirit of God, you move mysteriously. Elijah did not hear you in the wind or in the earthquake or in the fire, but in the gentle whisper. Teach us to discern the signs of your power in the gentle and the unspectacular.

The jailer woke up, and when he saw the prison doors open, he drew his sword and was about to kill himself because he thought the prisoners had escaped. But Paul shouted, "Don't harm yourself! We are all here!"

The wretched man would have been held responsible

if the prisoners had escaped. The usual punishment for jailers who let that happen was execution. But something had stopped the other prisoners from escaping. Everybody's chains had been loosened. Why didn't they flee?

Our modern minds are restless, Father. We want to know the reasons for everything. We analyse and speculate, we probe and argue. How easy it is, in the midst of our cleverness, to be the foolish ones who do not hear your word!

The jailer called for lights, rushed in and fell trembling before Paul and Silas. He then brought them out and asked, "Sirs, what must I do to be saved?" They replied, "Believe in the Lord Jesus, and you will be saved—you and your household." They spoke the word of the Lord to him and to all the others in his house.

"Faith comes from hearing the message, and the message is heard through the word of Christ." So Paul wrote to the Romans (10.17). Perhaps he remembered an occasion such as this.

The apostles took every opportunity to preach the word. Instead of thinking how they could turn this remarkable incident to their advantage, Paul and Silas used it as a means of proclaiming the kingdom of God. They were not concerned about their own safety. That was not high on their personal agenda. Their business was the Gospel.

Spirit, help us to discern your opportunity in all that happens to us; give us the words to witness to Jesus Christ when your moment comes.

At that hour of the night the jailer took them and washed

their wounds; then immediately he and all his family were baptised. The jailer brought them into his house and set a meal before them; he was filled with joy because he had come to believe in God—he and his whole family.

The first response of the jailer was to perform a simple ministry in washing the apostles' wounds (no miraculous healing this time!). Then he and his family immediately accepted the Gospel. They did not hesitate. Repentance, faith, baptism and the gift of the Holy Spirit brought them into the body of Christ.

We are members of that same body. We, too, have heard the Gospel. We have received baptism, forgiveness, and the Holy Spirit. Like the jailer and his family, we have shared in meals with our fellow-members. (Was that meal in the house a eucharist at which the jailer and his family received from the apostles their first communion?)

We are never alone in what we have to face. Even what looks like a disaster can become a blessing. We are one with each other in the church of Jesus Christ. "If one part of the body suffers, every part suffers with it; if one part is honoured, every part rejoices with it" (1 Cor 12.26).

Father, Son, Holy Spirit, renew in us the unity we have with you and with each other through our baptism. Enable us to minister to one another in your love and power, to bear one another's burdens, and to fulfil your will. May your church be filled with your glory and the Gospel of your kingdom proclaimed to those imprisoned in ignorance, selfishness and sin. Break down these gates, Lord God, beginning in me!

4 Philippians 4.4-7 Rejoice in the Lord always

Rejoice!
The summons echoes throughout the scriptures:
like a bell ringing
through books of prophets and apostles.
Because of the triumph at the cross
God is our Father,
and he spreads his protection over his people,
the overshadowing of his Spirit.
He who watches over us neither slumbers nor sleeps.
Those who love his name may *rejoice in the Lord always*.

Joy is a fruit of the Spirit.
It has nothing to do with my emotions,
or with my circumstances.
I can reject his gift.
I can turn in on myself and away from God.
My mind and my body can dominate me
in sorrow and bitterness
rather than in thanksgiving and joy.
But still the Father calls me
since I bear the name of Christ,
and I must answer.

I will say it again: Rejoice!
Paul repeated the summons.
Even though he was saying farewell
to his beloved church in Philippi
he could still share his joy with them.
If they rejoiced in the Lord as he did,
their spiritual fruit would be manifested to others

in gentleness and courtesy,
in thoughtfulness and forbearance.

Did they know the Psalmist's exhortation?
'Rejoice in the Lord and be glad, you righteous;
sing, all you who are upright in heart!'
(Ps 32.11).
Was it easy for them to rejoice?

What a contrast!
I am filled with anxieties.
What tomorrow will bring?
Will things be any better?
Will I really know within myself
the Lord's healing touch?

Peter wrote:
'Though you have not seen him, you love him:
and even though you do not see him now,
you believe in him
and are filled with an inexpressible and glorious joy,
for you are receiving the goal of your faith,
the salvation of your souls' (1 Pet 1.8).

Lord, I want to believe,
I want to love you.
I want to love you for yourself,
not just because I long to see healings
and to experience them myself.
I want to believe in you
without signs following.
I simply want to be your disciple,
for better, for worse,

for richer, for poorer,
in sickness and in health.

Jesus said:
'Do not worry about your life . . .
Seek first his kingdom and his righteousness,
and all these things
will be given to you as well' (Mt 6.25,33).

So the apostle could write:
Do not be anxious about anything,
but in everything, by prayer and petition,
with thanksgiving, present your requests to God.
And the peace of God,
which transcends all understanding,
will guard your hearts and your minds
in Christ Jesus.

Lord, forgive me for being anxious.
Take away all that troubles me.
Renew me afresh with your Holy Spirit.
and then I shall rejoice always.

PART 8

MINISTRY OF RECONCILIATION

Although Jesus Christ refuted the Old Testament concept of sickness as a punishment for personal sin (Jn 9.1–3), his teaching and his gifts of healing reveal that there is a close connection between human sickness and human disobedience to God. Our sins may not be the direct cause of our sickness (though they sometimes can be, in all sorts of unconscious as well as obvious ways), but the forgiveness of sins is part of the process of healing—the fundamental part, in fact, for unless we have responded in penitence to the message of the Gospel, we shall be setting up a barrier between ourselves and the salvation which comes from God through Jesus Christ.

This applies to all Christians, of course, not just to the sick. It applies to those who are called to exercise a ministry of healing as well as those who are recipients of the ministry. Those who pray for others with the laying on of hands need to be open to the Holy Spirit without the blockages of personal disobedience, which may cause them to stumble as they seek to minister in the name of Jesus Christ. Confession of sins, therefore, is one aspect of the ministry of healing which we dare not neglect—least of all in a book of prayers for healing.

But we can only confess our sins if we are able to recognise them as such; and this is also a work of the Spirit. It is he who convicts us of sin (Jn 16.8) and cuts us to the heart (Ac 2.37), moving us to repentance.

His gift of discernment enlightens our consciences so that we can recognise our faults. Only then can we truly confess our sins, ask for God's forgiveness through the cross of Jesus Christ, and seek his strength in being more obedient to him in the future.

So repentance is not just a strategy for healing or for self-improvement; it is allowing our deepest desires for God to come to the surface of our consciousness—especially our desires for the fruit of the Spirit: love, joy, peace, patience, kindness, goodness, faithfulness, gentleness, self-control (Gal 5.22). For changes can only come in our lives through the Spirit who dwells deep within us and who, when we allow him, works through our motives, feelings, thoughts and actions. As disciples of Jesus Christ we rely not on our own ability to get rid of sin, but on the power of God's love which has been poured into our hearts.

True, our desires for God are never perfect. We tend to be ambivalent. Sometimes we want to be more like Jesus Christ. Sometimes we prefer not to be changed! But our willingness to confess our sins and to ask in faith for the fruit of the Spirit is a test of our repentance. We show God that we want to love him, even if our loving is often only lukewarm.

There are many different ways of making a self-examination—a devotional exercise in which we open ourselves to the Spirit to convict us of sin. The following is a simple one based on our Lord's summary of the law (Mk 12.29–31). I have kept in mind that this is a preparation for the ministry of healing in which we may be ministers or patients. For it is then that our attitude towards those closest to us and our outlook on life generally will have a bearing both on our ministry to others or on our own physical, mental and emotional condition. At other times it may be necessary to include a more thorough review of our willingness to accept Christian responsibilities in matters relating to social justice, the struggle against racism, the promotion of peace, and so on, but I have not provided for that here.

A self-examination should not be agonisingly scrupulous or morbidly long: it should be brief but thorough. We commence by invoking the Spirit of God to enlighten our hearts and minds (e.g., by using a prayer such as 2.3). Then we read our aid to self-examination—in this case, the passage from the gospel—reflecting on the questions that rise in our minds as we apply its message to ourselves. It may be helpful to make a few notes.

SELF-EXAMINATION

One of the teachers of the law asked Jesus, "Of all the commandments, which is the most important?" "The most important one," answered Jesus, "is this: 'Hear, O Israel, the Lord our God is one Lord. Love the Lord your God with all your heart and with all your soul and with all your mind and with all your strength.' The second is this: 'Love your neighbour as yourself.' There is no commandment greater than these."

The words of Jesus bring together Deuteronomy 6.4 and Leviticus 19.18. The completeness of God's claim on our entire being is emphasised with the fourfold emphasis, *with all your heart . . . soul . . . mind . . . strength*. The second commandment, *Love your neighbour as yourself*, must not be taken to mean that there is, as it were, some love left over from our love of God which is available for ourselves and for others. This commandment explains what it means to love God unrestrictedly: it includes loving our neighbours who, with us, live and move and have our being in him.

The Lord our God is one.

The oneness of God means that the whole universe is under him and that there is nothing which is outside the scope of his divine will and power. No rival authority exists which can claim our allegiance or submission.

We can sin against the oneness of God:

(1) By resigning ourselves to some other influence. We can become cynical or fatalistic about our lives and those of others. We can succumb to failure and unhappiness, letting go of our faith and hope in God. We can give up the spiritual warfare against evil because we feel God cannot or will not help us.

(2) By thinking and acting as if God is concerned with only certain areas of our lives, and as if there are other areas where he is indifferent or impotent. Then we keep these latter areas cordoned off from him—such as our relationships with certain people, our ambitions, our sexuality, our use of money and possessions, or the control of our time.

(3) By worshipping other gods. The other gods are those people, ideas or things which replace the Lord as the primary focus of our devotion. They can be the man, woman or child who infatuates us, the pursuit of wealth, physical prowess, intellectual abilities, or hobbies that consume an inordinate amount of our time, attention and cash. We can even make a false god out of our spiritual experiences or our religious orthodoxy.

Now let us pause for a few moments and ask some questions.

What are the really big things in your life, and how

does your commitment to the Lord compare with them? From what areas have you wanted to keep God away? Where in your life is there fear, cynicism, defensiveness, obsession, fanaticism, hero worship, or addiction? Have you ever consented to be dominated by another person or group? Have you dabbled in the occult or demonism, or let your plans be shaped by astrology? Are you vain about your achievements or appearance?

Love the Lord your God with all your heart and with all your soul.

Jesus' words encourage us to aim at what we would otherwise not dare to imagine—a relationship of complete trust with God, coupled with a growing desire to belong more and more to him. This motive is to take root in the innermost depths of our being—in our heart and soul—so that everything in our lives springs from that union with him.

The essence of sin is withdrawal from God. "Go away from me, Lord; I am a sinful man!" (Lk 5.8). We fend off the Spirit's promptings, we keep our distance, we try to preserve our supposed independence. Breaking this commandment means brushing aside Christ's offer of sharing in his life with the Father in the Holy Spirit.

Questions: Have you put up barriers to God's love, particularly in those memories where such a feeling would cause pain? Have you tried to ignore spasms of anger or resentment against God, and never dared to be open with him about them? Are you prepared to let the Spirit purify and change your emotions, even if that means emerging with a different and more mature personality? Have you neglected to praise God and to thank him? Do you betray God by using his name in vain?

With all your mind

We do not always regard our minds as members of our bodies through which we are to love God. But it is sinful to let our thoughts dwell on matters which are not worthy of him, or to let our intellect detract us from commitment to Jesus as our Saviour and Lord. Many people are content with a careless agnosticism or a casual curiosity about Christian things, which shields them from the challenge of the Gospel. Others are intellectually lazy, not bothering to understand the faith of the New Testament.

Questions: Do you read the scriptures regularly? If there are particular doubts and difficulties, have you sought to talk about them with other wise Christians? Are you prepared to let God change your mind or turn your prejudices upside-down? Do you try to conceal your faith, or do you attempt to share it with others?

With all your strength

For everyone who believes in God, the indwelling Holy Spirit provides an inner strength. We are baptised in him and, if we are to love God wholeheartedly, we must be open to him at all times. Faith is sometimes difficult because the real God is hidden and mysterious, and our confidence in Jesus' love and power can be cast into doubt by evil forces or life's tragedies. We fall into sin when we give up the struggle and allow other things to take control of our lives. Then we lose touch with the love God has for us.

Questions: Where is the lukewarmness, the double-mindedness and the half-heartedness in your discipleship? When do you habitually give in to temptations? In what areas of your life do you avoid seeking the help of the Holy Spirit? Do you allow yourself to get discouraged—and to remain depressed—when things do not work out your way and when answers to prayer do not seem to be what you had expected?

Love your neighbour. . . .

Relationships with others fill up an enormous amount of our time and attention, and they are the means through which our love of God is tested and the reality of our faith is exposed. "We love because he first loved us. If anyone says, 'I love God,' yet hates his brother, he is a liar. For anyone who does not love his brother, whom he has seen, cannot love God, whom he has not seen" (1 Jn 4.19–20). Any self-examination must therefore be concerned with the attitudes we adopt and the way we behave towards others, starting with those closest to us.

Questions: What is your attitude towards your parents, your wife, your husband, children, relatives, friends, colleagues, casual acquaintances in everyday life, strangers? Do you need to accept forgiveness as well as offer it? Do you take others for granted? Are you quick to judge or to condemn others? Do you bear grudges? Are you aware of any prejudice within yourself because someone else belongs to another social class, a foreign country, or a different race? Do you allow others to have different opinions without despising them? Have you been demanding or perfectionist with those around you (especially a spouse or a child)? Have you been devious in your dealings with others? Have you ever been unfaithful to those dearest to you?

. . . . *As yourself*

Accepting ourselves as we are begins with the recognition that we are sinners in the sight of God. Once we have begun to do that, the Spirit will gently illuminate in our lives things which are unworthy of him and which will make us deeply ashamed and sorry.

Now part of the healing process is in realising that these feelings of shame and sorrow can become expressions of true repentance. They can show the Lord we want to be forgiven. What we need to do is to move beyond our feelings to an act of will in which we tell God that we want him to change our lives radically. It is at this point—where our feelings lead to the act of will—that the redemption which he offers us through the cross of Jesus Christ becomes real. In the days and weeks that follow these expressions of repentance we slowly realise that we have been given an inner awareness of his forgiveness and of his love for us.

Sometimes this awareness may be blocked by disturbances within ourselves. Self-hatred in all its forms is a crushing burden which is at the root of much ill-health. We are not always to blame for this, if the circumstances of our upbringing and development have seriously affected us and left us psychologically scarred. But we are to blame if wilfulness and self-pity prevent us from seeking the Lord's forgiveness and healing. Self-pity can easily go hand-in-hand with a lack of self-esteem and cause us to reject the good news that, "Since we have been justified through faith, we have peace with God through our Lord Jesus Christ, through whom we have gained access by faith into this grace in which we now stand" (Rom 5.1–2). If we are to love our neighbour as ourselves, then we must let the Spirit reveal to us how we hurt ourselves, whom God has created in his image and redeemed for the purposes of his kingdom.

Questions: In what ways have you gone against the life of God within you? Have you abused your body by overeating, lack of exercise, neglecting medical care, and addiction to alcohol, drugs or tobacco? Have you degraded yourself by feeding on the so-called entertainment that glorifies violence, racism, sexual immorality? Have you further degraded yourself by participating in any of these activities? Have you exhausted yourself by not recognising and honouring your limitations? Have you boasted of your independence and rejected your need of others? Have you neglected to seek help from God (perhaps through his people) when you knew you needed it?

At the end of such a self-examination, we may realise that we are guilty of sins we had not recognised before as well as the sins with which we were very familiar. In the name of Jesus Christ we ask the Father to forgive us and to fill us with his Spirit, so that we may be equipped to fight against temptations to sin again (e.g., prayer 2.2.)

We may find it helpful to seek advice about our failings. It is beyond the scope of this book to enter into a discussion about the value of Christian counselling and spiritual direction; but a talk with a wise Christian followed by a prayer, or an act of private confession to a priest or minister, is often where that kind of help begins, and then it becomes yet another step on the road to healing.

CONFESSION

Jesus discerned that in certain cases the person who came to him for healing needed an assurance of God's forgiveness or a warning not to sin again (Mk 2.1–12 and parallels; Jn 5.14). In these instances Jesus manifested himself as the Divine Healer who brings from God all that mankind needs for complete wholeness. "It is not the healthy who need a doctor, but the sick" (Mt 9.12.) So the healing he ministered included forgiveness of sins as well as physical healing or deliverance from evil. "God was reconciling the world to himself in Christ, not counting men's sins against them" (II Cor 5.18).

The gospels reveal that the Lord gave authority to his disciples to pronounce the forgiveness of sins in his name (Mt 18.18; Jn 20.23). Initially this was in calling men and women to repentance, faith and baptism, but eventually the apostolic church was guided to exercise that authority for members within its fellowship who fell into sin and sought a fresh reconciliation (I Cor 5. 1–5; II Cor 2.5–11). Interestingly the instruction about the confession of sins and forgiveness is linked in James 5.14–16 with the ministry of healing:

> Is any one of you sick? He should call the elders of the church to pray over him and anoint him with oil in the name of the Lord. And the prayer offered in faith will make the sick person well; the Lord will raise him up. If he has sinned, he will be forgiven. Therefore confess your sins to each other and pray for each other so that you may be healed. The prayer of a righteous man is powerful and effective.

Over the centuries this practice has come to be known as "going to confession" or, more usually nowadays, "the ministry of reconciliation." Although confessions of personal sins to any wise and discreet Christian have been common in every age (informally, at any rate), the usual custom has been to make one's confession to an ordained priest or minister using a prescribed form or "rite". Through the pastor, acting as a "confessor", the church exercises her ministry of reconciliation by declaring the forgiveness of sins (the "absolution") in the name of Jesus Christ.

Of course, the pastor has to be reasonably sure that the one who makes the confession (the "penitent") is repentant and wanting to amend his life in accordance with God's law. Sometimes the pastor may give the penitent some advice (the "counsel") before he absolves him.

In her teaching and discipline the church has traditionally made a distinction between the formal absolution declared by an ordained priest or minister and a prayer for forgiveness offered by a lay person. In the former case the pastor acts as one commissioned by the church to declare the forgiveness of sins in Jesus' name; in the latter case the one who prays acts as a fellow disciple interceding on behalf of another brother or sister in Christ.

The ministry of reconciliation is surrounded by regulations to safeguard both the penitent and the confessor. While confessions may be heard anytime and anywhere, they often take place in a church building, usually at the communion rail or in a place where the penitent and the confessor can be seen but not overheard. The penitent is expected to confess all known serious sins. Before pronouncing the absolution, the pastor may assign to the penitent a psalm, a prayer or a hymn to be said, or something to be done, as a sign of repentance and thanksgiving (the "act of penance"). The confessor is bound by church law never to divulge to anyone what has been said to him, or indeed to discuss it with the penitent afterwards. This is known as the "seal of the confessional".

I have reproduced in this section the rites for the ministry of reconciliation of the Episcopal Church of the USA and of the Roman Catholic Church.

The Episcopal Church's *Book of Common Prayer* (1972) contains two forms. Form One is fairly traditional and includes the absolution from the Church of England's *Prayer Book* (beginning, *Our Lord Jesus Christ, who has left power to his church*. . .) Form Two is modern. It includes a brief Bible reading, and the prayers underline the significance of the rite as a ministry in which the penitent is reconciled both to God and to the church.

It ends with a declaration of forgiveness which can be used by a deaconess or a lay person.

The rite from the Roman Catholic *Order of Penance* (1974) contains more detailed instructions for the priest and the penitent than I have given here. It also provides forms for penitential services.

EPISCOPAL CHURCH OF THE USA

THE RECONCILIATION OF A PENITENT

Form One

Penitent: Bless me, for I have sinned.

Priest: The Lord be in your heart and upon your lips that you may truly and humbly confess your sins; in the name of the Father, and of the Son, and of the Holy Spirit. Amen.

Penitent: I confess to almighty God, to his church, and to you, that I have sinned by my own fault in thought, word, and deed, in things done and left undone; especially. . . .
For these and all other sins which I cannot now remember, I am truly sorry. I pray God to have mercy on me. I firmly intend amendment of life, and I humbly beg forgiveness of God and his church, and ask you for counsel, direction and absolution.

Here the priest may offer counsel, direction and comfort. He then pronounces this absolution:

Our Lord Jesus Christ, who has left power to his church to absolve all sinners who truly repent and believe in him, of his great mercy forgive you all your offences; and by his authority committed to me, I absolve you from all your sins; in the name of the Father, and of the Son, and of the Holy Spirit. Amen.

or

Our Lord Jesus Christ, who offered himself to be sacrificed for us to the Father, and who conferred power on his church to forgive sins, absolve you through my ministry by the grace of the Holy Spirit, and restore you in the perfect peace of the church. Amen.
The Lord has put away all your sins.

Penitent: Thanks be to God.

Priest: Go (*or* abide) in peace, and pray for me, a sinner.

Form Two

The Priest and Penitent begin as follows:

Have mercy on me, O God, according to your loving kindness;
in your great compassion blot out my offences.
Wash me through and through from my wickedness,
and cleanse me from my sin.
For I know my transgressions only too well,
and my sin is ever before me.

Holy God, Holy and Mighty, Holy Immortal One,
have mercy upon me.

Penitent: Pray for me, a sinner.

Priest: May God in his love enlighten your heart, that you may remember in truth all your sins and his unfailing mercy. Amen.

The Priest may then say one or more of these or other appropriate verses of Scripture, first saying:

Hear the Word of God to all who truly turn to him.

Matthew 11.28 John 3.16 I Timothy 1.15 I John 2.1–2

Priest: Now, in the presence of Christ, and of me, his minister, confess your sins with a humble and obedient heart to Almighty God, our Creator and Redeemer.

Penitent: Holy God, heavenly Father, you formed me from the dust in your image and likeness, and redeemed me from sin and death by the cross of your Son Jesus Christ. Through the water of baptism you clothed me with the shining garment of his righteousness, and established me among your children in your kingdom. But I have squandered the inheritance of your saints, and have wandered far in a land that is waste.

Especially, I confess to you and to the church. . .

Here the penitent confesses particular sins.

Therefore, O Lord, from these and all other sins I cannot now remember, I turn to you in sorrow and repentance. Receive me again into the arms of your mercy, and restore me to the blessed company of your faithful people; through him in whom you have redeemed the world, your Son our Saviour Jesus Christ. Amen.

The priest may then offer words of comfort and counsel.

Priest: Will you turn again to Christ as your Lord?

Penitent: I will.

Priest: Do you, then, forgive those who have sinned against you?

Penitent: I forgive them.

Priest: May Almighty God in mercy receive your confession of sorrow and of faith, strengthen you in all goodness, and by the power of the Holy Spirit keep you in eternal life.

The priest then lays a hand upon the penitent's head (or extends a hand towards the penitent), saying one of the following:

Our Lord Jesus Christ, who offered himself to be sacrificed for us to the Father, and who conferred power on his church to forgive sins, absolve you through my ministry by the grace of the Holy Spirit, and restore you in the perfect peace of the church. Amen.

or this:

Our Lord Jesus Christ, who has left power to his church to absolve all sinners who truly repent and believe in him, of his great mercy forgive you all your offences; and by his authority committed to me, I absolve you from all your sins: in the name of the Father, and of the Son, and of the Holy Spirit. Amen.

The priest concludes:

Now there is rejoicing in heaven; for you were lost, and are found; you were dead, and are now alive in Christ Jesus our Lord. Go (*or* abide) in peace. The Lord has put away all your sins.

Penitent: Thanks be to God.

Declaration of Forgiveness to be used by a deacon or a lay person:

Our Lord Jesus Christ, who offered himself to be sacrificed for us to the Father, forgives your sins by the grace of the Holy Spirit. Amen.

ROMAN CATHOLIC CHURCH

RITE FOR RECONCILIATION OF INDIVIDUAL PENITENTS

The priest welcomes the penitent with one of these sentences:

May the grace of the Holy Spirit
fill your heart with light,
that you may confess your sins with loving trust
and come to know that God is merciful.

or

May the Lord be in your heart
and help you to confess your sins with true sorrow.

or

The Lord does not wish the sinner to die
but to turn back to him and live.
Come before him with trust in his mercy.

The penitent makes his confession using any form that is familiar to him. One form begins:

I confess to almighty God,
and to you,
that I have sinned through my own fault
in my thoughts and in my words,
and in what I have done,
and in what I have failed to do. . . .

If necessary, the priest helps the person to make an integral confession and gives advice on particular matters that may be troubling the penitent. He also invites the person to accept an act of penance (a prayer or a simple form of self-denial), if possible related to what has been confessed.

Then the penitent expresses sorrow using an appropriate prayer, such as one of these:

Lord Jesus,
you opened the eyes of the blind,
healed the sick,
forgave the sinful woman
and after Peter's denial confirmed him
in your love.
Listen to my prayer, forgive all my sins,
renew your love in my heart,
help me to live in perfect unity with my
fellow Christians
that I may proclaim your saving power to all
the world.

or

Father of mercy
like the prodigal son I return to you and say:
"I have sinned against you and am no longer
worthy to be called your son."
Christ Jesus, Saviour of the world,
I pray with the repentant thief
to whom you promised Paradise:

"Lord, remember me in your Kingdom."
Holy Spirit, fountain of love, I call on you with trust:
"Purify my heart, and help me to walk as a child of light."

Priest: God, the Father of mercies,
through the death and resurrection of his Son
has reconciled the world to himself
and sent the Holy Spirit among us
for the forgiveness of sins;
may God give you pardon and peace,
and I absolve you from your sins
in the name of the Father, and of the Son,
and of the Holy Spirit. Amen.

The Lord has freed you from sin.
May he bring you safely to his kingdom in heaven.
Glory to him for ever. Amen.

PART 9

SACRAMENTAL MINISTRY

The gospels contain a number of instances in which Jesus healed the sick by laying hands on them or by touch. "The people brought to Jesus all who had various kinds of sickness, and laying his hands on each one, he healed them" (Lk 4.40). One version of the commission which the risen Christ gave to his apostles contains the promise: "They will place their hands on sick people and they will get well" (Mk 16.18). And the early church continued that practice: "Paul went in to see him (the father of Publius) and, after prayer, placed his hands on him and healed him" (Ac 28.8).

Following biblical precedents, the laying on of hands became one of the ritual gestures used by the church in confirmation, in ordination, in commissioning and in absolving from sin, as well as in prayer for healing. The gesture indicates that the particular person on whom hands are being laid is the subject of the congregation's prayer, as they intercede with God to send his Holy Spirit to forgive, to bless, to authorise, and to heal. In later times the laying on of hands came to be defined in theological terms as a sacramental sign.

There is no record that Jesus personally anointed the sick with olive oil; he used spittle and clay (Mk 7.33, 8.23; Jn 9.29). His disciples used oil when sent out by him on their first mission: "They anointed many sick people with oil and healed them" (Mk 6.13). Anointing was accepted as an outward sign of the healing grace of God in the early church (Jas 5.14). This practice may have been related to the remedial use of oil for soothing and comforting the sick in the ancient world.

Like the laying on of hands, anointing also came to be a sacramental sign in initiation and ordination as well as in ministry to the sick. The prayers said over the olive oil when it is blessed for sacramental use remind us that it is an outward and visible sign of the inward anointing and power of the Holy Spirit.

Sacramental signs are ministered within the company of the local Christian congregation, community or group, who surround the sick with their prayers and uphold them with their faith (James 5.15). Sometimes that congregation may be no more than a few people—perhaps only the one who ministers to the sick person with the laying on of hands and anointing—but nevertheless they represent the Christian community gathered in the name of Jesus Christ to continue his healing work.

In ministry to the sick the laying on of hands with prayer is used freely in all kinds of situations—informally in a home as well as formally in a church service. Anointing with olive oil—unction, as it is sometimes called—is generally reserved for critical moments: when a serious illness has been diagnosed, at the beginning of a course of treatment, before an operation, and so on. In Anglican and Roman Catholic churches those who are to be anointed are sometimes advised to make their confession first (see Part 8).

The prayers in this section are taken from Anglican and Roman Catholic services for the sick. The Anglican prayers are from the Church of England's *Authorised Alternative Services: Ministry to the Sick* (1983) and the Episcopal Church of the USA's *Book of Common*

Prayer (1977). I have reproduced much of the Roman Catholic Church's *Liturgy of Anointing within the Eucharist* (1972) because I believe this material will be useful to other Christians when they exercise a ministry of healing within their own communion services. The notes at the end explain a few details.

CHURCH OF ENGLAND

The laying on of hands

In the name of our Lord Jesus Christ who laid his hands on the sick that they might be healed, I (we) lay my (our) hands upon you, N. May Almighty God, Father, Son, and Holy Spirit, make you whole in body, mind, and spirit, give you light and peace, and keep you in life eternal. **Amen.**

The anointing

N., I anoint you with oil in the name of our Lord Jesus Christ. May our heavenly Father make you whole in body and mind, and grant you the inward anointing of his Holy Spirit, the Spirit of strength and joy and peace. **Amen.**

The almighty Lord, who is a strong tower to all who put their trust in him, be now and evermore your defence, and make you believe and trust that the only name under heaven given for health and salvation is the name of our Lord Jesus Christ. **Amen.**

EPISCOPAL CHURCH OF THE USA

Form for the blessing of oil

O Lord, holy Father, giver of health and salvation: Send your Holy Spirit to sanctify this oil; that, as your holy apostles anointed many that were sick and healed them, so may those who in faith and repentance receive this holy unction be made whole; through Jesus Christ our Lord, who lives and reigns with you and the Holy Spirit, one God, for ever and ever. **Amen.**

The laying on of hands

N., I lay upon my hands upon you in the Name of the Father, and of the Son, and of the Holy Spirit, beseeching our Lord Jesus Christ to sustain you with his presence, to drive away all sickness of body and spirit, and to give you that victory of life and peace which will enable you to serve him both now and ever more. **Amen.**

or this

N., I lay my hands upon you in the Name of our Lord and Saviour Jesus Christ, beseeching him to uphold you and fill you with his grace, that you may know the healing power of his love. **Amen.**

The anointing

N., I anoint you in the name of the Father, and of the Son, and of the Holy Spirit.

As you are outwardly anointed with this holy oil, so may our heavenly Father grant you the inward anointing of the Holy Spirit. Of his great mercy, may he forgive you your sins, release you from suffering, and restore you to wholeness and strength. May he deliver you from all evil, preserve you in all goodness, and bring you to everlasting life; through Jesus Christ our Lord.

THE ROMAN CATHOLIC CHURCH

THE LITURGY OF ANOINTING WITHIN THE EUCHARIST

Reception of the Sick

1 *The priest welcomes the sick in these or similar words*:

(a) We have come together to celebrate the sacraments of anointing and the eucharist. Christ is always present when we gather in his name; today we welcome him especially as physician and healer. We pray that the sick may be restored to health by the gift of his mercy and made whole in his fulness.

(b) Christ taught his disciples to be a community of love. In praying together, in sharing all things, and in caring for the sick, they recalled his words: "In so far as you did this to one of these, you did it to me." We gather today to witness to this teaching and to pray in the name of Jesus the healer that the sick may be restored to health. Through this eucharist and anointing we invoke his healing power.

2 *A form of general confession is said by the priest and the congregation together, and the priest says an absolution.*

3 *Opening Prayer*

(a) Father,
you raised your Son's cross
as the sign of victory and life.
May all who share in his suffering
find in these sacraments
a source of fresh courage and healing.
We ask this through our Lord Jesus Christ,
your Son,
who lives and reigns with you and the Holy Spirit,
one God, for ever and ever. **Amen.**

(b) God of compassion,
you take every family under your care
and know our physical and spiritual needs.
Transform our weakness by the strength
of your grace
and confirm us in your covenant
so that we may grow in faith and love.
We ask this through our Lord Jesus Christ,
your Son,
who lives and reigns with you and the Holy Spirit,
one God, for ever and ever. **Amen.**

Liturgy of the Word

4 Suggested readings:

Old Testament	*New Testament*	*Gospel*
I Kings 19.1–8	Acts 3.1–10	Matthew 5.1–12
Job 3.3, 11–12,20–23	Acts 3.11–16	Matthew 8.1–4
Job 7.1–4,6–11	Romans 8.14–17	Mark 2.1–12
Job 7.12–21	Romans 12.1–2	Luke 10.25–37
Isaiah 35.1–10	I Corinthians 12.12–22, 24-27	Luke 10.5–6,8–9
Isaiah 52.13–53.12	I Peter 1.3–9	Luke 11.5–13
Isaiah 61.1–3	I John 3.1–2	John 9.1–7

5 ***Litany***

Let us pray to God for our brothers and sisters and for all those who devote themselves to caring for them.

Bless N. and N. and fill them with new hope and strength.

Lord have mercy.
Lord have mercy.

Free them from sin and do not let them give way to temptation.

Lord have mercy.
Lord have mercy.

Sustain all the sick with your power.

Lord have mercy.
Lord have mercy.

Assist all who care for the sick.

Lord have mercy.
Lord have mercy.

Give life and health to our brothers on whom we lay our hands in your name.

Lord have mercy.
Lord have mercy.

6 ***The Laying on of Hands***

in silence.

7 ***Blessing of Oil***

God of all consolation,
you chose and sent your Son to heal the world.
Graciously listen to our prayer of faith:
send the power of your Holy Spirit, the Consoler,
into this precious oil, this soothing ointment,
this rich gift, the fruit of the earth.

Bless this oil (+) and sanctify it for our use.

Make this oil a remedy for all who are anointed with it;
heal them in body, in soul, and in spirit,
and deliver them from every affliction.
We ask this through our Lord Jesus Christ, your Son, who lives
and reigns with you and the Holy Spirit, one God, for ever and ever.
Amen.

8 ***Prayer over the Oil***

Praise to you, God, the almighty Father.
You sent us your Son to live among us
and bring us salvation.

Blessed be God who heals us in Christ.

Praise to you, God, the only-begotten Son.
You humbled yourself to share in our humanity
and you heal our infirmities.

Blessed be God who heals us in Christ.

Praise to you, God, the Holy Spirit, the Consoler.
Your unfailing power gives us strength
in our bodily weakness.

Blessed be God who heals us in Christ.

God of mercy,
ease the sufferings and comfort the weakness of your servants
whom the church anoints with this holy oil.

We ask this through Christ our Lord. **Amen.**

9 ***The Anointing***

The priest anoints the sick person with the blessed oil. First he anoints the forehead, saying:

Through this holy anointing
may the Lord in his love and mercy help you
with the grace of his Holy Spirit.

Then the hands

May the Lord who frees you from sin
save you and raise you up. **Amen.**

10 ***Prayers after Anointing***

(a) *General*

Father in heaven,
through this holy anointing,
grant N. comfort in his suffering.
When he is afraid, give him courage,
when afflicted, give him patience,
when dejected, afford him hope,
and when alone, assure him of the support of your
holy people.
We ask this through Christ our Lord. **Amen.**

(b) *General*

Lord Jesus Christ, our Redeemer,
by the grace of your Holy Spirit
cure the weakness of your servant N.
Heal his sickness and forgive his sins;
expel all afflictions of mind and body;
mercifully restore him to full health,
and enable him to resume his former duties,
for you are Lord for ever and ever. **Amen.**

(c) *In extreme or terminal illness*

Lord Jesus Christ,
you chose to share our human nature,
to redeem all people, and to heal the sick.
Look with compassion on your servants,
whom we have anointed in your name with this holy
oil for the healing of their body and spirit.
Support them with your power,
comfort them with your protection,
and give them the strength to fight against evil.
Since you have given them a share in your
own passion,
help them to find hope in suffering,
for you are Lord for ever and ever. **Amen.**

(d) *In advanced age*

God of mercy,
look kindly on your servant
who has grown weak under the burden of years.
In this holy anointing
he asks for healing in body and soul.
Fill him with the strength of your Holy Spirit.
Keep him firm in faith and serene in hope,
so that he may give us all an example of patience
and joyfully witness to the power of your love.
We ask this through Christ our Lord. **Amen.**

(e) *For a child*

God our Father,
we have anointed your child N.
with the oil of healing and peace.
Caress him,
shelter him,
and keep him in your tender care.
We ask this in the name of Jesus the Lord. **Amen.**

(f) *For a young person*

God our healer,
in this time of sickness you have come
to bless N. with your grace.
Restore him to health and strength,
make him joyful in spirit,
and ready to embrace your will.
Grant this through Christ our Lord. **Amen.**

Liturgy of the Eucharist

11 *Eucharistic Prayer*

The Lord be with you.
And also with you.
Lift up your hearts.
We lift them up to the Lord.
Let us give thanks to the Lord our God.
It is right to give him thanks and praise.

Father, all-powerful and ever-loving God,
we do well always and everywhere to
give you thanks,
for you have revealed to us
in Christ the healer
your unfailing power and steadfast compassion.

In the splendour of his rising
your Son conquered suffering and death
and bequeathed to us his promise
of a new and glorious world,
where no bodily pain will afflict us
and no anguish of spirit.

Through your gift of the Spirit,
you bless us, even now,
with comfort and healing,
strength and hope,
forgiveness and peace.

In this supreme sacrament of your love
you give us the risen body of your Son:
a pattern of what we shall become
when he returns at the end of time.

In gladness and joy
we unite with angels and saints
in the great canticle of creation,
as we say:
Holy, holy, holy Lord, God of power and might,
heaven and earth are full of your glory.
Hosanna in the highest.
Blessed is he who comes in the name of the Lord.
Hosanna in the highest.

12 *Special Intercessions*

(a) Father, accept this offering
from your whole family,
and especially from those who ask for healing
of body, mind and spirit.
Grant us your peace in this life,
save us from final damnation,
and count us among those you have chosen.

(b) Remember also those who ask for healing
in the name of your Son,
that they may never cease to praise you
for the wonders of your power.

(c) Hear especially the prayers of those
who ask for healing
in the name of your Son,
that they may never cease to praise you
for the wonders of your power.

13 *Prayer after Communion*

(a) Merciful God,
in celebrating these mysteries
your people have received the gifts of unity
and peace.
Heal the afflicted
and make them whole
in the name of your Son,
who lives and reigns for ever and ever. **Amen.**

(b) Lord, through these sacraments
you offer us the gift of healing.
May this grace bear fruit among us
and make us strong in your service.
We ask this through Christ our Lord. **Amen.**

14 *Blessing*

May the God of all consolation
bless you in every way
and grant you hope all the days of your life. **Amen.**
May God restore you to health
and grant you salvation. **Amen.**
May God fill your heart with peace
and lead you to eternal life. **Amen.**
May Almighty God bless you,
the Father, and the Son, (+) and the Holy Spirit.
Amen.

NOTES

The blessing of oil (7) is omitted if this has already been done by a bishop or another priest.

Only the first part of the eucharistic prayer, up to the *Sanctus*, is printed here (11). In the Roman liturgy the second part of that prayer, which includes the words of institution, has provision for the insertion of special intercessions (12).

PART 10

A SERVICE OF PRAYER FOR HEALING

Services of prayer for healing demonstrate publicly that the congregation is concerned with the ministry of healing, and when healings take place they bear witness to the Gospel in a striking manner. Sometimes these services are specially organised on a regular monthly or two-monthly basis.

In this section I have composed a rite for such a service, including an outline of the sermon. Various practical details are added in the notes at the end.

Services like these should only be initiated when a congregation has been taught the biblical and pastoral principles behind such a ministry, and when at least some members have experienced sharing in prayer with the laying on of hands in small groups or in training courses. Arrangements also have to be made when individuals who have been prayed for require further counselling and care.

All those involved in the service should be encouraged to prepare for it by personal prayer and perhaps by keeping a simple fast.

Welcome

1 *As the ministers enter, an appropriate hymn or chorus may be sung.*

2 *The president welcomes the people and introduces the service.*

General confession and absolution

3 *He then invites the congregation to join in a general confession of sins with words such as:*

Let us confess our sin, in penitence and faith, firmly resolved to keep God's commandments and to live in love and peace with all men.

4 **Almighty God, our heavenly Father,**
we have sinned against you and against
our fellow men,
in thought and word and deed,
through negligence, through weakness,
through our own deliberate fault.
We are truly sorry
and repent of all our sins.
For the sake of your Son Jesus Christ, who
died for us,
forgive us all that is past;
and grant that we may serve you in newness of life
to the glory of your name. Amen.

5 *President:*

Almighty God,
who forgives all who truly repent,
have mercy upon us,
pardon and deliver us from all our sins,
confirm and strengthen us in all goodness,
and keep us in life eternal;
through Jesus Christ our Lord. Amen.

Collect

6 Heavenly Father,
your Son commissioned his disciples to heal
the sick,
and through the Holy Spirit you bestow gifts of
healing on his church.
Hear the prayers we offer in his name
and grant your healing
to those for whom we intercede
and those on whom we lay on hands (and whom
we anoint),
that together we may bear witness to the gospel
of salvation
and the glory of your kingdom;
we ask this through the same Jesus Christ our Lord.
Amen.

Ministry of the Word

7 First reading: Isaiah 35.3–6

Strengthen the feeble hands,
  steady the knees that give way;
say to those with fearful hearts,
  "Be strong, do not fear;
your God will come,
  he will come with vengeance,
with divine retribution
  he will come to save you.

Then will the eyes of the blind be opened
  and the ears of the deaf unstopped.
Then will the lame leap like a deer,
  and the mute tongue shout for joy.
Water will gush forth in the wilderness
  and streams in the desert.

8 *A hymn, a chorus, a psalm or an anthem may be sung between the readings.*

9 Second reading: Matthew 8.14–17

When Jesus came into Peter's house, he saw Peter's mother-in-law lying in bed with a fever. He touched her hand and the fever left her, and she got up and began to wait on him.
When evening came, many who were demon-possessed were brought to him, and he drove out the spirits with a word and healed all the sick. Thus was fulfilled what was spoken by the prophet Isaiah:

"He took up our infirmities
and carried our diseases."

10 *Sermon*

Outline

(a) "When Jesus came into Peter's house, he saw Peter's mother-in-law lying in bed with a fever." Where better to experience the ministry of healing than at home among one's family and friends? Many here in this congregation must have prayed for the members of their family at home when they were ill. What we are doing in church is but an extension of that ministry in the family of God. Jesus stretched out his hand and touched her. The laying on of hands is the formal way in which Christians follow his example in prayer for healing (refer to James 5.14–15).
(b) On other occasions, as when healing the demon-possessed, Christ spoke a word of command. We, too, when we pray for healing, seek to discern God's will and intercede for the sick with his authority. That is why we pray "in the name of Jesus Christ".

(c) God does not will sickness on any of us. In his kingdom "there will be no more death or mourning or crying or pain, for the old order of things has passed away" (Rev 21.4). But suffering and death are inescapably linked with this life—even for God's Son.

(d) We must never underestimate the influence of evil on sickness and disabilities (as well as everything else in our lives). We may not be personally responsible for many of the pains which come our way. Unjust suffering is one of the tragic mysteries we experience in this world. But we should be sure, when we seek God's healing, that we start by confessing our sins and asking for his forgiveness. That is where healing begins, and that is why we began the service with a general confession (see note 3).

(e) In New Testament times some illnesses were attributed to demonic possession which nowadays we know have physical and psychological origins. Instances of direct demonic troubling are rare. But we must be in no doubt about the reality of evil in our lives and must claim the victory of the cross for ourselves and for others.

(f) Because of the salvation Jesus Christ has won for us, we come to this service trusting in him.

He took up our infirmities
and carried our sorrows (Isa 53.4.)

Healing, like forgiveness, is a sign of his kingdom breaking through into our experience. It is not a reward for our faith—some of those Jesus healed did not appear to look on him as being anything more than a wonder-worker. We believe he is our Saviour, and so we submit to him knowing he is merciful and compassionate. Those of you who come forward for the laying on of hands should make that an act of personal re-commitment to him. The rest of us will also be re-committing ourselves to Jesus Christ as we pray for you. Together we will in a few minutes re-affirm our faith in the form used at baptisms.

(g) (A brief testimony—see note.)

(h) Isaiah prophesied to the Israelites in exile in Babylon that God would restore them in Sion and that the things they suffered would belong to the past. In one sense we are exiles in this world, for we seek a kingdom which is to come. But let us live for that kingdom in faith and hope now, and seek to serve the Lord in the power of his Spirit, looking for his healing in whatever manner he chooses to give it for the glory of his name.

> Then will the eyes of the blind be opened
> and the ears of the deaf unstopped.
> Then will the lame leap like a deer,
> and the mute tongue shout for joy.
> Water will gush forth in the wilderness
> and streams in the desert.

11 *The president invites the congregation to stand and reaffirm their faith*:

Do you believe and trust in God the Father, who made the world?

I believe and trust in him.

Do you believe and trust in his Son Jesus Christ, who redeemed mankind?

I believe and trust in him.

Do you believe and trust in his Holy Spirit, who gives life to the people of God?

I believe and trust in him.

12 *Hymn or chorus.*

Intercessions

13 *The minister or others lead the prayers. An opportunity is provided for members of the congregation to offer brief petitions for individuals (e.g., "For N., going into hospital next week"). The intercessions conclude with a form of corporate prayer.*

The laying on of hands

14 *Individuals are ministered to as arranged, while the congregation is led in prayers, songs and periods of silence.*

15 *If the laying on of hands is offered during a eucharist, the peace, the eucharistic prayer, the Lord's Prayer and the communion may take place here (see note).*

16 *The president leads the congregation in the Lord's Prayer:*

Our Father in heaven,
hallowed be your name,
your kingdom come,
your will be done,
on earth as in heaven.
Give us today our daily bread.
Forgive us our sins
as we forgive those who sin against us.
Lead us not into temptation
but deliver us from evil.
For the kingdom, the power, and the glory are yours
now and for ever. Amen.

Prayer

17 Heavenly Father,
you sent your Son
to proclaim the good news of your salvation
and to manifest your healing power.
Continue your gracious work among us
by the power of your Holy Spirit,
and grant that we who have received your forgiveness and healing
may live your gospel and manifest your kingdom
in all that we think and say and do,
now and always.
Through Jesus Christ our Physician and Saviour.
Amen.

18 *Hymn*

Blessing

19 *President:*

The Lord bless you and watch over you,
The Lord make his face to shine upon you and be gracious to you,
the Lord look kindly on you and give you peace;
and the blessing of God Almighty,
the Father, the Son, and the Holy Spirit,
be among you and remain with you always. **Amen**.

20 Go in the peace of Christ.

Thanks be to God.

NOTES

The numbers refer to the items in the service.

1 I have assumed that the service is being conducted in a church where the congregation normally follows a set rite. It will, therefore, seem similar to any other service. This similarity helps to demonstrate that a service with prayers for healing and the laying on of hands (and anointing) is as much part of the church's worship and life as, say, a baptism or a confirmation within a eucharist or any other service. The directions can obviously be modified for congregations who are used to a freer form of worship.

2 The term "president" is used to denote the worship leader. He (or she) should conduct the service with a relaxed authority, showing that he is in control of all that happens. It is better if the president does not get involved in ministry to individuals in 14 so that he can keep an overall view of what is going on.

3 Before introducing the general confession, the president reminds the congregation of the importance of repentance as a preparation for prayer for healing (see the sermon outline, 7d), and he allows a period of silence for self-examination. The confession and absolution can be transferred to later in the service if preferred (c.g., between 13 and 14).

4–7 The Ministry of the Word is the same as in any other service. If prayer with the laying on of hands is being offered within a eucharist, the Ministry of the Word will form part of that liturgy. Appropriate readings are to be found in most lectionaries (see Part 9).

7(g) A suitable testimony can be valuable, and the sermon is the obvious place in which to introduce it. It could be given by someone who has recently been healed, or by a member of the congregation who has a special responsibility for the sick—e.g., a doctor or a nurse.

11 The affirmation demonstrates that prayer for healing is offered in the faith of the whole congregation, not just in the faith of those who receive the ministry (see the preface to Part 8).

13 Participation in the intercessions by members of the congregation enables them to bring their own individual petitions for sick people they know personally into the service. It also strengthens the sense that this is a ministry of prayer by the whole congregation, not just of the few who lay on hands. Prayers 4.2 or 4.3 would be suitable; so would the litany in Part 9.

14 Unless they are elderly or crippled, those who ask for prayer with the laying on of hands should be encouraged to leave their seats and sit, kneel or stand with those who are ministering to them. For those who do not use spontaneous prayers, 3.5 and 3.8 are suitable, and the Anglican forms in Part 9. If possible, two people should minister to each individual (though this can only be done where members of the congregation have been trained for this). The time spent with each individual should be reasonably brief; this is not an appropriate occasion for a lengthy conversation. If further counselling is necessary, arrangements can be made to see them later. Care should be taken not to let the ministry to individuals go on for so long that it prolongs the service. If many come forward, then either more people should

be recruited to pray with them, or some should be asked to wait until the service is over. If anointings are given, they should be performed by those authorised to do so (see the preface to Part 9).

15 In a eucharist, the usual place for ministry to individuals (e.g., baptisms, confirmations, weddings and ordinations) is before the prayer over the bread and the wine and the receiving of communion—the act of communion setting the seal, as it were, on what has been done. And this is how the ministry to the sick is arranged in the Roman Catholic Liturgy of Anointing within the Eucharist (see Part 9). In practice, however, many congregations prefer to minister prayer with the laying on of hands after the distribution of the bread and the wine. This has the advantage that, if the ministry to individuals is prolonged, the rest of the congregation can finish the service and be dismissed without waiting until the end. The prayers in the Roman Catholic rite are very useful for any service of prayer for healing.

20 For further suggestions about these services, see my *The Lord is Our Healer*, chapter 10.

APPENDIX

THE SHAPE OF THE COLLECT AND SPONTANEOUS PRAYER

Liturgical prayers—that is, the formulas which were written long ago and which have come down to us in liturgical books—can do much to inspire and inform our own spontaneous prayers. We can learn from the way they address God and bring into their texts passages from the scriptures. We can discern the inbreathing of the Spirit in the things they say as they praise God, confess sinfulness, and express hopes and needs. Many Christians find these prayers like guide-ropes in the dark, when they are going through dry periods in their devotional life and they feel there is nothing they want to say to the Lord.

We have already seen how litanies (Part 4) and thanksgivings (Part 5) can be used as a framework for our prayers. Now we will examine how the collect can help us when we pray freely. To do this we shall have to analyse the shape of the collect and see how it presents requests to God.

The *collectio*, to give the prayer its Latin title, appears in some of the oldest liturgical books and probably came into use as early as the fifth or sixth century. It derived its name either from the custom of using this form of prayer when people "collected" together for worship, or when the one who led a congregation "collected" in a general prayer the petitions which had already been offered to God either corporately or silently. In its Latin version it was usually brief and rhythmical; translated into English it could be longer and more elaborate. Many of the collects in the *Prayer Book* were translated from the Latin by Archbishop Thomas Cranmer (1489–1556) and they are much admired for their literary qualities.

The shape of the collect was influenced by the manner in which people make formal requests to one another when asking for favours. This can be illustrated by an imaginary letter:

1 Dear Bill,
2 You kindly offered to help me erect my shed in the garden when the parts were delivered.
3 They have now arrived, and I would be grateful if you would come round tomorrow and give me a hand in putting it up.
4 I want to use it for my tools and gardening equipment as soon as possible.
5 Thank you for making this offer. Yours ever, John.

Note the various stages in this letter:

1 The customary greeting.
2 The reminder that Bill had offered his help when required.
3 The request itself.
4 The reason why the request is being made.
5 The grateful rounding off of the letter.

Now compare the numbered stages of that letter with this collect, which comes from the service in the Church of England's *Ministry to the Sick* (1983) for "The Laying on of Hands with Prayer, and Anointing, at the Holy Communion":

1 Heavenly Father,
2 you anointed your Son Jesus Christ
with the Holy Spirit and with power
to bring to man the blessings of your kingdom.
3 Anoint your church with the same Holy Spirit,
4 that we who share in his suffering and his victory
may bear witness to the gospel of salvation;
5 through Jesus Christ our Lord, who lives and reigns
with you and the Holy Spirit, one God, for ever and
ever.

The content of each stage is worth noting:

1 The petition is addressed to the First Person of the Holy Trinity. This follows the pattern of the Lord's Prayer and of other New Testament prayers. In collects generally the attributes of God are used according to the scriptural references and the nature of the petition. In this particular collect, reference is made to the baptism of Jesus Christ, when the voice of the Father was heard from heaven; so God the Father is addressed as "heavenly." If the collect had invoked, let us say, the mercy of God, before going on to request his forgiveness, it might have begun, "Merciful Father," or "God of compassion."

2 In the narratives of the baptism of Christ (Mt 3. 13–17; Mk 1.9–11; Lk 3.21–22; Jn 1.32–34) there are references only to the Holy Spirit's descending on Jesus as a dove; there is no mention of "power." That comes later, in Luke's account of Jesus at Nazareth (4.16–30), in some of the healing miracles (e.g., the power going out of Jesus when he was touched by the sick woman, Lk

8.46), in the promise of the Spirit to the disciples (Ac 1.8), and in the experience of the ministry of healing in the apostolic church (e.g., Ac 3.13). My point is that the use of the phrase, "Holy Spirit and power," followed by "the blessings of your kingdom," recalls not just the baptism of Christ but a cluster of New Testament passages which link together the gift of the Spirit, the proclamation of the gospel of the kingdom, and the miracles of healing both in the ministry of Jesus and in that of the apostolic church.

3 The prayer's request is that the congregation gathered for the service should receive the same Spirit who was sent by the Father to Jesus and to the apostolic church. The same verb is used as in stage 1—"anoint."

4 "We who share in his suffering and his victory" echoes Romans 8.17: "If we are children, then we are also heirs —heirs of God and co-heirs with Christ, if indeed we share in his sufferings in order that we may also share in his glory." The collect follows the apostle in believing that the suffering of the sick is a means of union with Jesus as well as a prelude to sharing in his victory. It does not directly ask for healing; that request comes later in the service. Instead, it asks that those who pray might "bear witness to the gospel of salvation"—that as the Spirit strengthens them, their share in Christ's suffering and victory might be the means of drawing others to faith in the salvation which the Father offers. "The gospel of salvation" comes from Ephesians 1.13: "You also were included in Christ when you heard the word of truth, the gospel of your salvation."

5 Collects end with an ascription to the Holy Trinity. In this case the full text is not printed. All that appears is, "Through Jesus Christ our Lord," after which the congregation says, "Amen." But according to liturgical

custom, the longer version may be added (see note 8 on page 32 of *The Alternative Service Book 1980*.) As we have seen, most ancient collects are addressed to God the Father. In modern times there has been a tendency to write collects addressed to Jesus Christ (2.4, 2.7, &c.), and a few to the Holy Spirit (e.g., 2.3, 3.4, &c.) But however they are addressed, they are composed with a devout awareness that when we pray, we are speaking to the Three Persons of the Godhead.

Although the collect belongs to our Christian liturgical tradition, its roots can be traced back to songs and prayers in the Old and New Testaments. Take, for example, Psalm 88.1–2:

> O Lord, the God who saves me,
> day and night I cry out before you.
> May my prayer come before you;
> turn your ear to my cry.

As in the collect, the psalmist offers his petition in confidence because of what the Lord has done in the past.

A similar pattern is discernible in Romans 15.5–6:

> May the God who gives endurance and encouragement
> give you a spirit of unity among yourselves in Christ Jesus,
> so that with one heart and one mouth
> you may glorify the God and Father of our Lord Jesus Christ.

And in Hebrews 13.20–21:

> May the God of peace,
> who through the blood of the eternal covenant
> brought back from the dead our Lord Jesus,
> that great Shepherd of the sheep,

equip you with everything good for doing his will,
  and may he work in us what is pleasing to him,
through Jesus Christ,
  to whom be glory for ever and ever. Amen.

In each of these passages God is addressed as the one who has already spoken to and acted for his people and who can be relied on completely for his faithfulness. In this sense, then, they are ancestors of the collect form.

To pray *in* and *through* the Holy Spirit is, of course, the essence of New Testament teaching on the nature of prayer. Although it is an exhortation rather than a prayer, the Trinitarian pattern emerges in the epistles in a number of places, for example, in 2 Corinthians 13.14:

May the grace of the Lord Jesus Christ,
  and the love of God,
and the fellowship of the Holy Spirit
  be with you all.

And in Jude 20–21:

But you, dear friends, build yourselves up in your most holy faith and pray in the Holy Spirit. Keep yourselves in God's love as you wait for the mercy of our Lord Jesus Christ to bring you to eternal life.

The collect, through its structure, simply reflects this truth. As we learn how to use it as a model for our own prayers, we shall find that it helps us in various ways.

(1) It will help us not to be too long. Too much free prayer tends to ramble on, until those who listen to it are not thinking of the Lord any more but wishing the prayer would get to the "Amen"! We don't have to be as brief as the traditional collect; but with its shape in our minds, we can compose our prayers so that they move from

beginning to end in a logical sequence. Many of the prayers in Parts 1–3 are intended to illustrate this. For example, 3.5, which asks God for a fresh anointing of the Holy Spirit on those who are to engage in the ministry of healing, begins with a reference to the sending of the Holy Spirit by the Father on the Son at the river Jordan, like the collect from the *ASB* just quoted. But then the request in what I have called stage 3 is extended into a prayer for healing, and in stage 4 it draws on the hope expressed in the biblical text printed at the top of the page.

(2) It will help us seek the inspiration for our prayers from the scriptures. Since stage 2 of the collect usually refers to something God has done or said, this starts us off with a reference to a biblical text, and as the rest of the prayer unfolds it may continue to echo words and phrases as well as promises and concepts from the scriptural passages associated with it. After reading the Bible either privately or in a group, we shall find ourselves using what we have been studying in the prayers. In liturgical books like the *ASB*, the collects for the Sundays and other days of the year often reflect the scripture readings appointed for those occasions.

(3) It will help us to participate more fully in liturgical worship. We shall become more sensitive to the richness of the formal prayers used in church, and we shall begin to see in them much that encourages us and guides us. Even the formulas we have been used to hearing for years acquire a new freshness through our experience of using them as the framework for our own devotions.

Eventually we shall get so used to the collect that we adapt its shape for our prayers without thinking about it. Of course, we don't always have to use it. Often we shall pray in other ways, as the Spirit leads us. But we can go back to the shape of the collect, especially on those occasions when we need to pray but lack the inspiration; and then we shall frequently discover our words being guided in new directions as we make our personal contribution to the liturgical tradition of which we are a living part.